Acting with Adler

Also by Joanna Rotté

Scene Change: A Theatre Diary—Prague, Moscow, Leningrad

Acting with Adler

Joanna Rotté

EXPANDED AND UPDATED EDITION

Foreword by Isaac Butler

APPLAUSE
THEATRE & CINEMA BOOKS

APPLAUSE
THEATRE & CINEMA BOOKS

Bloomsbury Publishing Group, Inc.
4501 Forbes Blvd., Ste. 200
Lanham, MD 20706
ApplauseBooks.com

Distributed by NATIONAL BOOK NETWORK

Copyright © 2000, 2024 by Joanna Rotté
Originally published by Limelight Editions in 2000.

Library of Congress Cataloging-in-Publication Data

Names: Rotté, Joanna, author. | Butler, Isaac, writer of foreword.
Title: Acting with Adler / Joanna Rotté ; foreword by Isaac Butler.
Description: Expanded and updated edition. | Essex, Connecticut :
  Applause Theatre & Cinema Books, 2024. | Includes bibliographical
  references.
Identifiers: LCCN 2024021944 (print) | LCCN 2024021945 (ebook)
  | ISBN 9781493085118 (paperback) | ISBN 9781493085125
  (ebook)
Subjects: LCSH: Adler, Stella. | Acting. | Method acting.
Classification: LCC PN2062 .R68 2024 (print) | LCC PN2062
  (ebook) | DDC 792/.028--dc23/eng/20240624
LC record available at https://lccn.loc.gov/2024021944
LC ebook record available at https://lccn.loc.gov/2024021945

∞™ The paper used in this publication meets the minimum
requirements of American National Standard for Information
Sciences—Permanence of Paper for Printed Library Materials,
ANSI/NISO Z39.48-1992.

To my son, Masashi Rotté

Acknowledgments

I'm grateful for every single word of interest ever expressed concerning my work on the teachings of Stella Adler. That includes the words of students, colleagues, friends, family, acquaintances, and strangers. I'm fortunate in having kind and energetic persons in my life who over the course of more than a year continued to encourage me in writing the new chapter for the new edition. I'm particularly and abidingly thankful to Karen Remmler, Christine Herbes-Sommers, Saxon Trainor, and Janet Fishman for reading the new material and giving me helpful feedback.

I thank Scott Balcerzak for his endorsement. I thank Rose Malague for conversations concerning the impact and importance of Stella Adler's teachings to this day. I most heartily thank Isaac Butler for his very smart, very helpful, very generous Foreword to the new edition.

Now and into the future, I express appreciation for Tom Oppenheim. As Stella Adler's grandson and president of the Stella Adler Studio, he steadfastly keeps the Adler artistic sensibility not only alive and well but progressively evolving.

There would have been no new edition without Chris Chappell, senior editor for Applause Books at Rowman & Littlefield. I first encountered Chris in a phone call during the COVID-19 pandemic. Though we've still not met in person, I've experienced his good sense, good judgment, and goodwill throughout our correspondence and communication. A deep bow of thanks to Chris and all the gracious staff at Rowman & Littlefield who have contributed to creating a new *Acting with Adler*.

In the original book or first edition, I acknowledged my editor Linda Elliot, publisher Mel Zerman (president of Limelight Editions), and adviser Glenn Loney. They are no longer with us. I offered heartfelt thanks to Ellen Adler for her generosity in allowing me to quote from the classes of her mother. She is no longer with us. I honor them all.

There are not enough words of gratitude in the English language to thank my son Masashi Rotté to whom this book is dedicated. He was a youngster when I wrote the original. There were days that I, as a single parent, neglected him to write it. He fended for himself and let me be. Now he is a thriving, adventurous adult, and I am a mother most fortunate.

Contents

Foreword

Isaac Butler

It is tempting to tell you right now—you, as in the person reading this, and now, as in *this very moment*—to skip the following and get right to the actual book. I am an inveterate skipper of forewords, preferring to read them at the end of my experience with a book, if at all, and I feel like a bit of a hypocrite having my words physically bar your progress. And besides, you hold in your hand the most useful and best-written guide to the ideas and techniques of Stella Adler, a book that is the next best thing to studying with the late, great genius of acting herself. But let me try, with my allotted space, to tell you a little bit about Stella and her significance to me and to the culture at large.

Stella Adler's life spanned most of the twentieth century—she was born in 1901 and died at the end of 1992—and in that life many threads wove together. She was a first-generation child of Jewish immigrants, an actor, a woman, and part of the American Left during a century that saw huge changes for all of these communities. She was born into the closest thing New York Jews had to royalty—the family and theater company of Jacob Adler, the greatest Yiddish Theatre actor manager of his day. She entered the family business at the age of five and discovered an interest in all things scholarly when her father demanded she go to the public library at the age of nine to research the ideas of Baruch Spinoza in order to play the Jewish philosopher as a child. In her early years, she performed in many plays, learned French, romanced Sergei Prokofiev, married a gifted musician, and bore a daughter, Ellen. But this order to her life quickly fell apart; her father suffered a stroke in 1920 which hampered his acting career for the final years leading up to his death in 1926. Due to both restrictions on Jewish immigration and the drive to assimilate into white America, American Yiddish culture, which had enjoyed a renaissance, was slowly dying in New York. Adler's husband struggled with mental illness and proved unreliable as a partner (they would divorce in 1930), and acting had begun to lose its sense of purpose. These struggles mirrored the chaos of the world around her. The world order ushered in by the invention of the nation-state had collapsed in the battlefields of Verdun, of the Somme, of Ypres, and in the fields of Flanders. By the end of the 1920s, global capitalism would crumble in the stock market crash of 1929.

She found renewed purpose for both her life and the art of acting through the teachings of Konstantin Stanislavsky. She studied Stanislavsky's ideas twice, once in the 1920s—from his students Richard Boleslavsky and Maria Ouspenskaya at the American Laboratory Theatre in New York—and then from the man himself in Paris in 1934. What she learned from them is detailed wonderfully by Rotté in the book you're about to read, so rather than risk redundancy, I want to instead detail a bit of that sense of purpose that she discovered, of the vision of the world, and art, and the actor's place in both that would become her lodestar after her fateful encounter with Stanislavsky's ideas.

It is a vision that I find incredibly moving, and one that has proven quite useful to me as I struggle with my own place as an artist in a world whose systems also feel on the verge—or perhaps in the midst—of collapse.

To theorize about acting is to theorize about the nature of being human. Stanislavsky's ideas about acting—which began in a dedication to specificity over type, naturalism over ostentation, unification of ensemble over star turns— all reflected his deep-rooted values and belief in the dignity of the individual. His early years had been spent under the rule of Czar Alexander II, who freed the serfs and attempted to bring some liberalizing reforms to Russia, but his career as an actor, director, and impresario began in earnest during the reign of Alexander the Liberator's son. Alexander III, nicknamed "The Colossus," was a highly reactionary autocrat who tried to claw back as many of his father's reforms as he could and believed in the absolute power of his monarchy. When Stanislavsky's Moscow Art Theater began in 1897, fewer than one in five Russians could read, and theater was subjected to multiple censorship regimes. One governed what people could read, another what could be performed, a third was controlled by the Church, and a fourth governed what could be performed for the working classes. The attempt to regulate information was one of many ways that the state attempted to control the individual.

Stanislavsky responded to all of this by insisting that human beings are not simply defined by their rank, or their type, but rather have an individual consciousness, made up of observed behavior, which could be captured and replicated by actors. That consciousness and behavior is shaped by the world around them, what Stanislavsky called

"the given circumstances": the time, place, class structure, religion, and so on in which they find themselves.
Stanislavsky demanded that those actors serve something
greater than themselves, that they dedicate their very souls
to the art form they practiced, the company that employed
them, and the ensemble in which their work would feature. Stanislavsky and his partner, Vladimir Nemirovich-
Danchenko are the ones who coined the phrase "There
are no small parts, only small actors." Their expectation
was that whether you played a spear carrier or Hamlet, you
worked as hard on your role as you possibly could. One of
Stanislavsky's great innovations was the imposition of what
he called "stage ethics." Actors had to show up on time, to
be humble, to treat each other well, to know their lines on
time. To do anything less was a crime against art.

It was this relentless drive for perfection, for doing right
by the art form to which he had dedicated his life, that
eventually led Stanislavsky to develop what he called the
"system." The "system"—often styled with a lowercase
"s" and quotation marks to symbolize its always unfinished
nature—was a series of techniques, ideas, and approaches
that enabled actors to be inspired and in character on
demand. It was the first comprehensive approach to acting
that treated the inner mechanism of the actor along with
the outer, that looked into the soul and the mind for the
materials that would allow a character to be born.

Stanislavsky's great genius was an ability to import and
adapt ideas from a wide variety of sources, and this was
as true with his values as it was for anything else. The
first source of his ethics was Russia's great novelist, Leo
Tolstoy, who wrote in a treatise called "What Is Art?" that
art is "the manifestation of feelings, conveyed externally."

Tolstoy argued that art is "a means of communion" whose highest goal is to unify humanity through expressing the "loftiest and best feelings people have attained in life." Tolstoy believed that the artist could infect the spectator, transmitting the former's feelings to the latter, creating communion. All three of these terms—infect, transmit, communion—would recur throughout Stanislavsky's writing for the rest of his life. In *An Actor's Work on a Role*, for example, Stanislavsky later wrote that when performing, "the artist . . . conveys the life of the human spirit itself that flows like an underwater current under the external facts" of a play.

A second source was the critic Vissarion Belinsky, best known as the man who coined the term "intelligentsia" to describe a new class of thinkers and artists that stood outside of Russia's highly stratified system of social rank. He viewed artists as missionaries. Their job was to elevate the world by highlighting its poetic nature, but he meant the poetic nature of *the real world*. Since we live in an age of science, art's task is to describe the world accurately, or as he put it, "in all its truth and nakedness." Art was a way of bettering society, but its tools were different from science, or economics, or politics. The artist, he wrote, should not "be the instrument of this or that party or of that sect . . . but the instrument of the profound and secret thoughts of a whole society, the instrument of aspirations of which they may only as yet be dimly aware."

Both of these influences came together in a third—Stanislavsky's lifelong Russian Orthodox faith, and his association with a group of Russian Orthodox quasi-dissidents known as the Old Believers. The Old Believers do not map easily onto our own theological and political geography.

In some ways they were progressive; in others they could easily be read as reactionary. They wanted the Russian church to return to ways of operating that predated the Czarist reforms that began in the eighteenth century with Peter the Great. But they also were anti-authority; valued industriousness, reliability, sobriety, and education; and had stringent ethical standards. All of this would influence Stanislavsky, who was a teetotaler, sedulously faithful to his wife—even Isadora Duncan failed to woo him!—and ran his theater and his family's textile empire for decades simultaneously. Old Believers also felt that human beings had a "Holy Task," a life's higher purpose, unique to each person, which must be accomplished in an ethical, just, and selfless manner.

These values are the subtext of Stanislavsky's "system," the hidden foundation that supports the whole edifice. What the Americans would bring to these ideas in the 1930s was a utopian belief that a better world was possible, one that art could help bring about, and a Jewish immigrant intellectual perspective. With the notable exception of Elia Kazan, all of the original major American teachers of Stanislavsky's ideas in the mid-century were Jews: Stella Adler, Harold Clurman, Lee Strasberg, Robert Lewis, and Sanford Meisner. All of them took pieces of Stanislavsky's "system" and made them central to their own pedagogy, but Stella's teachings were the ones in which the ethical roots of the "system" found their deepest purchase.

While her personal life was far stormier than Stanislavsky's, Stella had a keen sense of ethics when it came to art. She believed that art is something great, something that we must earn the right to be a part of. Art was special, a rarified and refined expression of the human condition, and actors—if they did the work, if they dedicated themselves to the art—could reach beyond the prison of the self and into something *more*. She also brought to the study of theater an almost Talmudic attention to text. Her script analysis classes, legendary during her lifetime, much mythologized since, dug into a script through a deep examination of the writer's entire body of work, the existing critical discourse around the text, and a granular attention to language. In her archives at the Harry Ransom Center at the University of Texas, I was able to see how she prepared for these lectures. Using blown-up xeroxes of play scripts so that each piece of paper had perhaps three to four lines of text on it, Stella would annotate with a keen eye for the hidden meanings of even the most innocuous words. We would all be so lucky as to have our work read by someone with her attention to detail.

Adler's vision of art is one that demands we be citizens of the world. It requires us to engage fully in our holy task of art-making with the totality of our being, and use this conglomeration of intellect, imagination, physicality, and research to transcend ourselves, to not just *be* but to *become*. It's an immensely moving vision of what a life could be, and it undergirds her techniques just as fully as it did Konstantin Stanislavsky's. But for those of us who never studied with her, there's been one rather large hurdle to understanding both her vision and her techniques: she was a terrible writer.

Three major books exist under her name. Two of them, *Stella Adler on Ibsen, Strindberg, and Chekhov* and *Stella Adler on America's Master Playwrights*, are adapted from her script analysis lectures and crackle with genius. They are stimulating, charming, profound. *The Technique of Acting*, however, is a leaden and miserable reading experience. It feels reluctant, as if she did not really want to write it. She's in good company here. Lee Strasberg's posthumous *A Dream of Passion* is also awkward and obtuse; Stanislavsky's behemoth *An Actor's Work* (known in the United States as the trilogy *An Actor Prepares*, *Building a Character*, and *Creating a Role*) is nearly as torturous an experience to read as it was for him to write.

How lucky we are, then, to have Joanne Rotté, who studied with Adler and then was one of the few actors to have been directed by her in a short-lived theater company. Here, in lucid, practical, illuminating chapters that combine anecdote, aphorism, and real-world examples, you will find Adler's technique brilliantly described. It is a book that is not only useful to actors but to anyone who cares about the interpretation of text and how art can contain, transmit, transform, and be transformed by ideas. Stanislavsky realized that theater could be a unique vessel for conveying the human spirit, a spirit whose light was often dimmed under the repressions of his time. We do not live under the Czar—or, thank goodness, Josef Stalin—but there are always forces seeking to dim the light inside of us. Adler instead wanted us to cultivate that light, and to illuminate the essential, eternal truths of our lives with it. This book, then, is also a set of matches, waiting for the kindling of the reader. Please enjoy the light, and the heat, that results from your encounter with it.

Preface to the Second Edition

With this new edition of *Acting with Adler*, I want to welcome a new generation of actors into the pragmatic and soaring world of Stella Adler. May you, young actors, discover how Stella's teachings can overcome the confusion of building a character and playing a role. I'm also pleased to roll out a red carpet for veteran actors—indeed, for all performing arts people, including playwrights, given Stanislavsky's assertion that understanding acting will help one's playwriting. For those of you who have already visited Stella Adler's world, I invite you to come again, perhaps with a sense of understanding action more deeply or refreshing the presence of Adler's principles in your work. Stella always said it takes ten years to grasp the technique. It took me at least that long, plus the endeavor of writing a book about it.

I offer myself as a reliable guide to Stella Adler's art of acting. It was nothing but good fortune that Stella trusted me with access to a literal closetful of her syllabi, class notes, and audio recordings. As far as I know, I'm the only person, of those who studied with Stella, who wrote a book covering her approach to acting and made a career of teaching theatre. I wrote *Acting with Adler* almost exclusively from firsthand sources, using Stella's materials, my notes from classes, and my memories.

Acting with Adler was published in 2000 by Limelight Editions and happily has not gone out of print. Stella's daughter Ellen Adler wrote the Foreword for the original edition. From Limelight, the book eventually migrated through two other arts publishers until finding a home with Applause Books at Rowman & Littlefield. More than a year ago, during a phone conversation with Chris Chappell, Applause Senior Editor, he proposed doing a new edition. Initially, I was thinking, "Oh, man, what would that look like in my aging life?" Then I considered what Stella meant to me and how her progressive mind and unfailing faith in artistic culture influenced the values I evolved through a career in theatre: prepossessing combo-values like humanistic feminism, aristocratic socialism, and secular Buddhism! And I remembered how early on, giving classes in script analysis at Villanova University, I could hear Stella's inflections and phrases coloring my voice, until one day, realizing I was no longer sounding like Ms. Adler, I acknowledged the achievement of independence from the teacher! And that, entirely, was Stella Adler's unselfish aim for all her students: independence or nondependence. With Chris Chappell's encouragement, I determined to give it a try: that is, to write a Preface, which is what you're reading now; to write a new chapter with an eye toward the future; and to ask Isaac Butler to write a new Foreword.

My ideas of theatre are beholden to two giants—Stella Adler, of course, and Harold Clurman, co-founder of the Group Theatre (1931–1941). They were, for me, *kalam-itra*-like teachers, that is, spiritual friends. I was fortunate to meet them both in a period of history when the work of astonishing American playwrights like David Rabe, Ntozake Shange, and Sam Shepard was flourishing; and experimental work was being born at The Living Theatre and the Open Theater, and via Robert Wilson; and Off-Broadway work, like that produced by Joe Papp at the Public Theater where I got my Equity card, gave me and my comrades good reasons to stay in New York and not take off for the West Coast or try for a part on the soaps at the network studios.

When I met Harold and then Stella, I was young. Luckily, I listened to them. Together, they understood theatre as a living art created through interdependence and capable of effectively influencing the insight of human beings and the advance of human culture. That's a way of saying what theatre came to mean to me. Holding this view, I wrote a new chapter for *Acting with Adler*, "The Development of the Artist Human Being." The new chapter lays down a path for the actor from Artist to Actor-Citizen to Artist–Human Being. It's a path that Stella implied and that I've tried to make explicit in the new chapter. Pursuing the path is to conduct a revolution upon oneself. The chapter also provides a perhaps unexpected picture of what I believe Stella Adler would be teaching if she were alive today. And the chapter ends with a call to action for the creation of a national theatre.

I came of age in a marvelous moment for the making of powerful, penetrating theatre. May the upcoming generation of theatremakers find cause to express the uniqueness of their time and place. And as the flower of theatre is in danger of withering, may all performing arts–oriented and performing arts–appreciative people bring wisdom and compassion as well as talent and discipline to the project of a healthy American theatre.

Acting with Adler

Introduction

You must travel ten thousand miles to find the person who can give you a technique that makes you secure.[1]

From 1949, when the Stella Adler Conservatory of Acting opened in New York City, until the death of Stella Adler in 1992, new students came to her each fall to test their histrionic talent and their commitment to the way of life of an actor. She introduced them to the historical fact that they had selected a profession draped in various approaches to training. She recalled, for example, the initiation rites common in the early days of this century, when she earned her own passage onto the stage:

> In those days they called it the business of acting. They never called it an art. Persons who wanted to act walked around and went to matinees, and from that they went and knocked on the back doors of stock companies asking, "Is there any room for me?" . . . The young actors hung around and listened. They carried a spear, a sword, and they played a monk, an old man, a young man, a little comedy. They learned a scale, a range. They watched other actors at work. . . . But these approaches are no longer available and this kind of

1

hit-or-miss method is inadequate to meet today's
theatrical demands.[2]

To replace the old way of learning in the field, Adler
offered the prospect of studying a technique of acting in a
studio before entering the theatrical marketplace.

She conceived the idea of a studio as a haven in which
students could become persons equal to the times in which
they lived and actors equal to the demands of contemporary
theatre. Students would be taught to cultivate the habit
of looking at themselves not as persons scooped along by
the manners of convention, but as souls actively pursuing
a creative life. The studio would be a refuge in which students would be allowed, even encouraged, to fail, so that
they need not be pressured, or their work crippled, by a
requirement to succeed. It would be a shelter in which
they would receive the guidance and support of a teacher
who would care less about the result of their work than the
effort put into it, and who would care about *them*. It would
be an environment in which students could gain security in
a technique, giving them the craft to solve any artistic problem that might confront them in their profession. In short,
training in a studio would be the preparation most likely to
ensure an actor's artistic survival.

The technique that Adler taught was based on her own
life experiences and observations, on her work as an actor
and director, on the influences of her parents, Jacob and
Sarah Adler (stars of the Yiddish Theatre), and primarily on
the teachings of Konstantin Stanislavsky—variously called
the Method, the Stanislavsky System, or simply the System.
Adler knew the System not as a fixed set of rules or codified
way of performing. It was not something invented by a

human being and therefore culturally limited. Rather, it was one man's understanding of the logic of Nature applied to an art form. As such, the System, like Nature, Adler considered open and available, meant to be applied by all actors to all acting tasks.

But she did not expect the System to be applied carelessly. The result of carelessness, which Adler witnessed in theatres, was the "mumbling, stumbling young actor without vocal, physical, or emotional discipline." She said that Stanislavsky had insisted upon a respect for the training of the actor along traditional histrionic lines, including voice projection, refined diction, and agility of the body. But in Adler's opinion, the instrumental aspect of the actor—his whole vocal and physical tuning—had tended to be neglected by Method training (in favor of emphasizing emotional tuning). One of her tutorial aims in stressing the development of the actor's instruments was to prevent misuse of the System.

Adler's ultimate tutorial aim was the actor's independence. If the actor truly understood and absorbed the System, he would contact his own creative powers and rise above any explicitness of the System. Adler had herself absorbed Stanislavsky's concepts and imaginatively reworked them; she was no longer able to say precisely which aspects of her method were his and which were exclusively hers. Thus, while Adler's students were learning a technique of acting and acquiring good working habits she was behaving as a guide, helping them develop the strength to reformulate the System themselves and go on their way. The role she set for herself was "not to teach, but to lessen the anguish" of learning.

But Adler *was* a teacher, and a great one. She was the

only American teacher of acting to have studied with Stanislavsky and also with Brecht, or to have acted under the direction of Reinhardt (as Catherine Canrick in Irwin Shaw's *Sons and Soldiers*, 1943–44). She was the teacher of two of America's most effective male screen actors, Marlon Brando and Robert De Niro. And she was my teacher, within a year of the night that Harold Clurman introduced us in the lobby of the Martin Beck Theatre, saying, "This is Joanna Rotté. She's a doctoral candidate in my American Theatre class at CUNY." Stella drew herself up and replied, "Yes, but what does she know?" Sensing that Stella Adler had something remarkable to teach, I became her student.

For forty-three years, Adler taught her own, always evolving interpretation of the psychological-realism-based Stanislavsky System. What may be little known is that Adler was interested in other styles besides psychological realism. Finding the acting style (that is, the manner of expression) appropriate to a piece was central to her advanced teachings. In Play Analysis she explored the differences in acting style needed for Brecht, Beckett, and Pinter based on their differences in language. She knew what to do with the double entendre style of Restoration comedy—though she recommended that American actors leave the uniquely British humor of Restoration plays to the British! Her studio offered a course in Shakespeare, focusing on the problems of verse and complicated language. She called on the ancient Greeks for imbuing the actor with size and a feel for eternity. In Advanced Character she taught heightening, which is to build up the external qualities of the character, making them larger than everyday reality or even larger than conventional stage reality. Also in Advanced Character she introduced fantastical realism, turning the students toward

Maeterlinck for creating non-human characters like Milk, Bread, Fire, or The Dog. For Scene Study class she assigned and analyzed the intensely colorful ("already heightened") characters of Tennessee Williams. But in terms of a personal aesthetic, she was drawn in the wake of her love for Chekhov to poetic realism.

When my class graduated in the 1970s from our two years of Conservatory training—there were seven of us remaining from a starting group of forty—we formed an acting company and persuaded Ms. Adler to come out of directorial retirement. (She had last directed Conservatory actors in the late 1950s, in a production of *Alice in Wonderland*.) Stella chose to direct us in Thornton Wilder's *The Happy Journey to Trenton and Camden*, using silences, repetitive motion, and four chairs on a bare stage. She solicited others to direct us in the craziness of Eva Le Gallienne's *Alice in Wonderland*, Murray Schisgal's *The Chinese*, and Sean O'Casey's *Bedtime Story*. We were especially physical in our roles, changing at the least our way of walking and talking, and Stella delighted in our accents and external characterization.

Adler's appreciation of style does not mean that she rejected the System in any way. Acting style was not some technique to replace the System but was a melody arranged around it. So, for Adler, to act was to do an action truthfully—in a style—in given circumstances. With all her natural theatricality and taste for style, Adler's pedagogy never veered from a sense of truth.

Adler brought this sense of truth into her way of life; but hers was not a literal honesty. She was an imaginative observer. She disdained reporting mere facts and instead spoke about the nature of a thing. Some years after I had graduated from the studio, on the birth of my son in Japan I sent her an announcement card noting the baby's statistics. She wrote back, "If 3100 grams, 50 cm is what he is, then it seems to me he is like a big dish of oatmeal." Adler was not interested in the outline. She had the audacity to look inside a person; and she had the perspicacity to sense what an actor needed at a given moment to open up his inside to the outside.

After my second year at the studio, I visited Stella's home in the Hamptons, where I met her feisty live-in Russian housekeeper, Ludmilla. The story was then circulating that Stella had slapped Ludie across the face for talking disrespectfully and that Ludie had slapped her back. Stella apparently had appreciated the gesture. She reveled in spontaneity and was theatrical to the core.

In the cooler months Stella dressed in black or camel, and when the weather turned warm, in beige or off-white— colors setting off the platinum of her hair, the black mascara and liner smudging her eyes, and the ruby red of her lipstick. She was tall and well formed, with full breasts that she clutched when impassioned. Her blouses were silk and V-necked. There was nothing of the puritan about her, nor the dowager. On occasion after lunch, she would return to class with her trousers unzipped. She stood on artistic principles and not social conventions.

Stella didn't just come into a room; she made an entrance, wafted on the scent of eau de cologne. And she didn't walk, she glided, reaching from one piece of furniture to another or from the arm of one person to the next, always extending, pausing to stroke or squeeze or grasp something or someone as she went.

She was flirtatious, with an earthy sexiness. She was

funny and could be ditsy in the manner of Lucille Ball, whom she resembled, particularly when her hair was curled and colored strawberry-blond. Still, she radiated glamour—although up close one could detect a false eyelash slipping or her hemline drooping or a run in a nylon stocking. Her third and last husband, the physicist and science-fiction writer Mitchell Wilson, once said, "Stella dresses for the ninth row" (the critics' row in the theatre). On evenings when she would be going directly from teaching to dinner and a show, she would change her clothes at the studio, and on occasion I would be the one to tease and comb her tousled hair. Left to herself, she might have arranged only the front and left the back in a tangle.

Although she was unaccustomed to featuring her intellect, Adler was a studious reader. Wilson had considered her a scholar. Had she been born in Europe, I believe, she would have been recognized as an artist-intellectual. In an interview over tea served at her Fifth Avenue apartment by a maid in white cap and apron, Stella told me that she had asked a psychiatrist friend if reading more than one book at a time indicated neurosis; she had books of all sorts at her bedside—fiction, biography, plays, criticism, history.

When teaching, Stella sat posture-perfect in a high-backed chair of carved wood and red velvet resembling a throne, situated down right of a low stage. Her notebooks and scripts lay on a table before her, and her reading glasses hung around her neck. We students faced front, occupying ascending rows of theatre seats. When any of us would overcome our timidity, our anxiety of going onstage for an exercise, she would turn and watch with total involvement. In three years of training, I never entirely lost a fear of showing her my work.

Stella's respect for acting was so intense! When responding to a student's work, she would begin her feedback
haltingly, searchingly, thoughtfully, licking her lips, until
she found the heart of what she wanted to say, and then she
would zero in with fervor and authority. Her observations
and suggestions could bite, but they were neither glib nor
personal. Ultimately, they were dead-on. I liked watching
her teach: her immersion, her impeccable acting craft, her
confidence in the striking nature of her own good looks. I
liked her drama, her gestures. I liked looking at the crook
in the bridge of her nose that must have been the result of
a nose fixing gone awry.

All Stella had to say was, "The children," and she could
cry authentic tears. Fake acting or a dense student would
upset her. "Shyness is vulgar," she would shout when no
one jumped up to work. "Keats died at twenty-eight! What
are you waiting for?" She was a formidable teacher—students quit the Conservatory in numbers—yet she was
pleased when graduates would visit the studio, bringing her
chocolates or flowers. Usually people brought roses, but
daisies made her eyes glisten.

Stella was the queen at home as much as within the
studio; she believed in the aristocracy of the artist. Her
Manhattan apartment, featured in the February 1985 issue
of *Architectural Digest*, was resplendent with French and
Venetian chandeliers, furniture upholstered in shades of
cream and gold, a grand piano, photos of her actor parents,
roses or irises in crystal vases . . . and cupids. Statues and
knickknacks of cupids in postures of adoration or flight
were everywhere, to the extent that Mitchell Wilson once
said that when he had begun courting Stella he had felt as
if he were being watched.

She also believed in work. While rehearsing Wilder's *Happy Journey*, we actors inadvertently made a mess of the backstage area. The room was way too small for our cast of five, with costumes and makeup, books and gear, but still, we hadn't helped the situation by strewing coffee cups, cigarette butts, used tissues, and garbage in general. On the weekend of dress rehearsal, Stella came backstage to greet us, and stayed to teach a lesson. To say that she was appalled would not be overstating. She called for a broom, a bucket of suds, a scrub brush, and a trash bin. As soon as we had gathered up the garbage, Stella got down on her seventy-three-year-old hands and knees to scrub the floor. She wouldn't let any of us help. With immense discomfort, we watched her. I wanted to grab away the bucket, and instead I cried. Someone begged her to stop. When the floor was clean, she said, "The actor is the sanity of the theatre. It's up to you to keep the theatre healthy."

Adler inherited high standards from her actor parents, and in turn she expected us to inherit them from her. In casting the Wilder play, she gathered our band of actors in a circle and assigned the roles. When only one role remained (that of the Mother, which was the leading role) only one actor remained—me. In fact, I was too young to play the Mother; I lacked life experience. Stella looked at me and at the other actors and said, "I guess we'll have to bring back Suzanne to play the Mother." I stared at her in horror and disbelief, and she said, "On second thought, maybe Joanna could play the part, because she just looked at me with murder in her eyes and this mother is a real killer." Stella had been testing my mettle for the role, and by virtue of spontaneous passion I passed her test. At the same time, for goodness' sake, this was a Thornton Wilder mother, not Mother Courage or some Greek mother like Medea or Clytemnestra! But then, it was Stella's way to exhort us to elevate our acting above "street level" to the uplifted level of the stage. So in that sense, even a homey Thornton Wilder mother should be seen as a mother capable of murder for the sake of her children.

One day during rehearsals of *Happy Journey*, when I was home with the flu, rather than cancel rehearsal Stella came with the cast to my apartment in Chelsea, where I lay on the sofa as we worked through the script. A year later, when Stella's beloved husband, Mitchell Wilson, died, she wouldn't leave the bedroom of her Fifth Avenue home. We visited her, keeping watch in groups and taking turns at her bedside. She told me, "I always thought I was strong. And I used to say about someone like you that they're strong. I'll never use that word again. It's not a word for a woman." I was afraid she had broken. But she had not. Stella survived the death of Wilson and threw herself again into the work of teaching.

I enjoyed a close relationship with Stella, but always as her student, an actor under her direction, or a graduate of her Conservatory. Even as I revered her, I was more connected to Harold Clurman, who had been her second husband and had introduced me to her. Harold had been my professor at the CUNY Graduate Center and I had become his frequent theatre, opera, ballet, and film companion. On one of our outings, having a brandy at the Russian Tea Room, on my way to the rest room I passed a table where Stella was seated with friends. She caught my arm and said, "Who do you belong to: him or me?" Though a smile graced her face, I sensed she was seriously asking me to choose, and I felt torn. I respected and loved them both and wanted to belong to them both.

Now I belong to neither Stella nor Harold, though each gave me a treasure beyond compare. I have written this book to give something back. Besides representing my gratitude, *Acting with Adler* may fill a vacuum. Adler's own book, *The Technique of Acting*, published in 1988, is a slim introduction to her method. Her other book, *Stella Adler on Ibsen, Strindberg, and Chekhov*, published in 1999, seven years after her death, compiles the extraordinary insight she brought to script interpretation. The only other record of her actor training is a PBS video, "Stella Adler: Awake and Dream!," part of the *American Masters* series, featuring Adler teaching at her studio in Los Angeles in the 1980s.

Stella Adler's outreach was far and her influence wide. She taught at her Conservatory in New York City, where students came by the hundreds and where New York University students attended classes for college credit. She taught Play Analysis outside her Conservatory for the New York professional theatre community. At various times, she taught at the New School for Social Research, at the Yale School of Drama, and in the summer at her studio in Los Angeles. Her acting, directing, and teaching work with the Group Theatre throughout the 1930s might also be considered; that is, in terms of her effect upon the teachings and (indirectly) the students of, and the actors directed by, Morris Carnovsky, Harold Clurman, Elia Kazan, Robert Lewis, Sanford Meisner, Lee Strasberg, and all the other acting teachers, actors, and directors taught by them. Certainly, the stage and film work of her own former students—including Alvin Ailey,

Warren Beatty, Candice Bergen, Peter Bogdanovich, Marlon Brando, James Coburn, Robert De Niro, Nina Foch, Teri Garr, Melanie Griffith, Lauren Hutton, Harvey Keitel, Jayne Meadows, Sidney Pollock, Anthony Quinn, Jerome Robbins, Cybill Shepherd, Elaine Stritch, Leslie Uggams, and Henry Winkler—has demonstrated an artistry worth emulating.

To write this book, I worked with my own class notes taken over three years as her student and as an actor under her direction. I also worked with more than 5,000 pages of unedited lesson plans covering twenty-five years of Conservatory classes that Ms. Adler gave me to use. I organized this material into a step-by-step presentation of the techniques that Stella Adler taught, meaning that the book bears my own structuring and interpretation of Stella Adler's teachings. My intention has been to provide a thoughtful yet visceral view of what it was like to study with Stella Adler at her studio. My hope is that you, the reader, will feel in the end that you have studied with Stella Adler too.[3]

NOTES

[1]Unless otherwise noted, all quotations throughout the text are the words of Stella Adler, taken from classes she taught at the Stella Adler Conservatory in New York City from the mid-1950s to 1980.

[2]Stella Adler, "The Art of Acting (The Actor's Needs)," *The Theatre II* (April 1960): 16–17.

[3]For additional biographical information on Stella Adler, please see my "Stella Adler: Teacher Emeritus," *The Journal of American Drama and Theatre*, fall 1999, 63–79. For a relevant article on Harold Clurman, please see my "Questions of Life and Art: Recollecting Harold Clurman," *New Theatre Quarterly*, fall 1992, 241–248.

A Note on Usage

Since I have chosen to use the singular "actor" throughout, the problem of pronouns has arisen. Rather than repeatedly encumbering you with "he or she or they"s and "his or her or their"s and "himself or herself or themselves"s, I have followed Ms. Adler's own custom and used the masculine singular pronoun in reference to "actor" in the generic sense. Also, this pronoun choice readily distinguishes "she" and "her" as referring to Stella Adler. Most assuredly, the choice is not meant to give preference to the masculine over any other gender and most especially not over the feminine. In a few places where it follows logic to use the feminine pronoun, I have.

CHAPTER I

The Development of the Actor

During my first term of study at the Stella Adler Conservatory of Acting, the class of forty students, of which I was one, followed a process of self-development. We were instructed to define for ourselves, not for Adler or for one another, the standards by which we had so far measured ourselves, and to assess the results of having accepted these standards. We were then asked to compare our standards with those necessary for an actor, the measure of which Adler gradually unfolded. By the end of our first term, equipped with Adler's principles and techniques to travel the actor's path of artistic, spiritual, and physical development, my classmates and I had found a direction and begun the journey.

ARTISTIC STANDARDS

The actor must be in complete control of his artistic development for as long as he lives.

In the first few days of class, Adler challenged us to question the validity of our own values, beliefs, and lifestyles to the profession of acting. She charged us to get rid of institutionalized opinions and to stop being victims of any sort of rumors and gossip purveyed by "ignorant people." Intending that we elevate our own, she asked us to abandon conventional standards, which, she insisted, were those of advertisements. In accordance with what her own teachers, particularly her parents, had demanded of her, she expected us to create our own standards.

Having pointed out that we would need to make choices in pursuing an acting career, Adler posed questions: Craft or comfort? Content or glamour? Spirit or material? The answers to the questions marked the differences between being an artist and being a merchant. She was distilling the ethics of the profession, inspiring us to regulate our lives in such a way that we would put all our integrity, confidence, and activity into the training, and put all distractions aside. She warned us that:

- We had not chosen an easy or ordinary profession.
- We should not expect approval or understanding from our families or from society.
- When we were ready to work professionally, we should not look to the producer or even to the director for assistance.

She urged us to become realistic about the hard edges on the world of theatre.

> Know that the director may want to exploit you. Whatever his attitude, understand that he may have chosen not to care. But always give your best by offering your creative self. Take the position of a servant, in service to the production, but do not forget that the servant estimates the master [the

director and/or producer]. Know with whom you
are dealing.

It was not entirely a picture of servile struggle that Adler
presented. She took care to balance a sense of severity with
potential rewards, explaining, for example, that an actor's
life, however misunderstood or ridiculed, is not necessarily
lonely. "Artists are together," she said, "helping each other's soulfulness to emerge."

Reaching the artistic standards Adler proposed depended
upon cultivating three qualities: confidence, knowledge of
the tradition, and a capacity for growth. The obstacles to
attaining her standards were overestimating the value of a
salary and misunderstanding the meaning of success.

While Adler conceded that each of us had to earn a living, she was concerned that we should become actors more
eager to learn and grow than to sell something. Also, she
pointed out that to any one of us success might mistakenly
mean being hired all the time, or applauded, or mentioned
in the newspapers. Adler wanted us to define success not
in terms of acclamation but in terms of gaining control of
our own destiny. She said that the only reality the actor can
depend upon, always, for as long as he lives, is feeling that
his work is good.

> If he does not feel it [that his work is good], then
> no money, applause, or symbol of success can give
> it to him. That feeling, which is confidence, must be
> established in him. When he has it, he will not need
> anybody else. He will collaborate with the director,
> but he will never say "Help me!"

Adler believed in a universal motivation, overriding any lure of fame or money and regardless of background or temperament, for someone's becoming an actor. But she first related what her father had to say on the subject: "To become an actor you have to have three reasons. Usually, the three reasons are: You don't want to get up early, you don't want to work, and you're afraid to steal." Adler's reasoning was singular: you become an actor because everyday reality is not enough for you.

Working in the theatre, which Adler considered not a job but a way of life, the actor can transcend the limitations of everyday reality. The actor can express himself freely and continue developing for as long as he lives. Adler believed that the actor would go on developing, once having the tools, the training, and the discipline to do so, even if the stage were taken away: "To grow: that is his deepest and truest need when he says, 'I want to be an actor.'"

Adler insisted that we set off a struggle within ourselves, to fight for our own human development. She congratulated us for being creatures full of animal vitality. At the same time, she warned us not to offer our vitality to theatrical agents, nor do commercials, nor spend our time going where the money was. She nudged us away from the easy or lazy path, since, in her vocabulary, lazy was just another word for stupid. She told us that our inner nature, much more so than our body, needed our protection. She expected us to put ourselves in touch with what so-called civilized persons must do in order to be truly civilized. Then we would come to see how creative work, with or without material payment, would make us feel good as human beings.

Adler's means of inner human development was exposure

to the world's five thousand years of cultural tradition, which had turned the animal into a human being.

> The stream of dramatic literature that runs from Ancient Greece to the gulf of the twentieth century, all the regional and national characteristics, all the languages, the shifting and changing styles, the different periods of time, the levels of society, the mores and morals of passing years, the cut of clothing from generation to generation, the different furniture, the very sound of the music in the air, the evolution that has changed the earthenware mug into a paper drinking-cup: these are the inheritance of the theatre student today.

By rooting himself in tradition, the actor can grow to the psychic size necessary to be civilized. It is, indeed, the actor's obligation to the profession to resist the tendency, however fashionable, to be "little," by which Adler meant

> resisting the urge to protect his little emotion as he comfortably sits in his little chair, in his little blue-jeans, and stares at his little world that extends from right to left.
>
> If the actor confines himself to the beat of his generation only, if he is bound within the limits of his street corner, alienated from every object or period that does not contain his own pulse, then the result is a disrespect for the world in general, and a foreignness to anything around that is not immediately recognizable as part of his everyday habits.

Our responsibility was to absorb the centuries' worth of theatre and culture that had preceded us, upon which our growth depended. We had to study the differences between then and there and here and now. We had to explore, for example, the differences between eighteenth-century people and ourselves in manners, education, and leisure activity. We had to take the knowledge we had gained of other societies and feed it to our psyches, so that we could imaginatively experience other times and places as if living there. We could then recognize the value of other cultures and customs, and we could have a historical standard of judgment against which to measure our own artistic efforts.

Adler judged it difficult in an industrialized country, where identical things are manufactured in the hundreds of thousands, to appreciate the intrinsic value of another culture, an object, or even a human being. In modern times in the United States, she noted, one does not necessarily readily acknowledge that a hand-stitched lace handkerchief passed down from one's great grandmother, which perhaps took an old Italian peasant woman several hours to make, is entirely different in value from a piece of Kleenex. Regardless of the confusion over values in modern society, Adler expected us to consider our work not temporal but connected to a tradition, and ourselves not disposable but valuable.

To help us recognize our worth, Adler invoked Stanislavsky's understanding of the value and glory of the individual actor. She explained that his System replaced the conventional or generic image of what an actor is with the actor's infinite capacity for feeling "Nobody is me, so I am great." Simply, the individuality of any actor marks him as incomparable with all others. With Stanislavsky, it became possible for people who never thought they could to become real actors. As Adler declared, "Although Laurence Olivier might stand on his head, he cannot be you. Only you have the privilege to be you." She encouraged us to dispense with fantasies of becoming the best actor there is, and concentrate on becoming the best actor each of us could be—which is where our triumph would lie.

Adler recalled her reply to *Time* magazine's question as to whether or not her former student Marlon Brando was a great actor: "We will never know. He has greatness in him, but there is not an actor in the world who knows whether he is great or not unless he plays the great parts." Extending back into the theatrical tradition is the way to reach one's best. And to find one's best, the reach has to be as wide as it is long.

> You are never a great conductor unless you conduct the Bs—Bach, Beethoven, Brahms. You are never a great composer unless you write in the symphonic form. You are never a great writer unless you write in the poetic form. As an actor, your aim must be equally as great.
>
> You have to stretch. You have to know the differences between Roman, Romanesque, and Romantic, and between Odets, Strindberg, Shaw, and O'Neill. You have to learn to deal with all the things that are comedy, that are fast, that require your entire equipment. You must try for musicals, and for classical and psychological drama. You need not fear experimenting, or enlarging your

equipment, in order to be ready to fit into a variety
of plays and styles.

Adler insisted on the actor's obligation to reach for a psychic size worthy of the stage. She considered it the actor's job not to discuss, argue or philosophize about life, but to experience it. She said that the difference between the actor and the other members of the large cultural group is that history is alive within the actor. While the intellectual says how something is, the actor does it, lives it: "Only if you own Denmark [by imaginatively living in Shakespeare's given circumstances] can you be Hamlet." Only by experiencing the size of the inheritance of modern humanity can the actor grow into an artist with a vision and a style uniquely his or her own.

The Principle is
AIM HIGH.

SPIRITUAL STANDARDS

The beginning of being in the theatre is not to have a wall between yourself and another human being.

Adler reminded us that few professions provide the privilege of taking the platform and having an audience. The actor (along with the priest, the politician, and the teacher) has that privilege and the obligation to be deserving of it.

She wanted us to make of ourselves good material for acting: stageworthy people able to handle the depth and breadth of modern drama. Today's theatre, as she understood it, is concerned with epic ideas, centering on a search for identity by characters having no god, no king, and no Communist Party to tell them who they are and how to live. It is through thinking about, and experiencing the magnitude of, the eternal questions of life, to which there are no easy answers nowadays, that the modern actor becomes articulate onstage. It is through acting dramatic situations containing large ideas that the actor becomes a medium of influence. The modern actor has the responsibility to "give people something that will change them."

Adler asked us each to become "a giant for expressing large ideas" by detaching from everything commonplace. She said we could not afford to be ordinary in our souls. We needed courage to relinquish the desire for popularity, self-discipline to be unconcerned with material rewards, and faith to overcome fear. We needed to transform any personal characteristics inappropriate to our occupying an influential position in society. Timidity, for example, was likely to pull us down and make us petty. Embarrassment was a cultural posture and shyness was vulgar. Whatever qualities might hinder us from being the boss over our own destiny were problematic for the profession of acting.

Our preparatory work on ourselves was to be done quietly in private, with care and concentration. Our daily ritual was observance of the world. Our discoveries were our secrets, not to be bandied about as topics for idle conversation but to serve as material for creation.

Adler expected self-discipline, and that demanded sacrifice. Actually, in her mind, the discipline was the sacrifice. She cited the lesson of John Gielgud, who said, "First I was conceited, then I was emotional, now I work." She quoted a former student, actor Larry Blyden, who said that he had gone out from the Conservatory quite cocky, got a part, got fired, and then said to himself, "I'm going to work now, and in the future I'll never not know why I'm being fired."

Adler's fundamental spiritual standard was to extend oneself outward to the maximum degree. She was not asking us to give up our lives; rather, she was advising us to open ourselves up to the experience of *love*, by going out of our way to do things for others, even little things. The practice of generosity, she said, in addition to being basically human, benefits the actor professionally, enabling him to reach the audience verbally, physically, and intellectually. Developing ease in giving, the actor can enjoy a kind of love affair with the audience, letting the magnanimous stage personality emerge.

Adler held up Michael Chekhov, whom she considered the greatest actor of the twentieth century, as a model of magnanimity. She recalled the graciousness of his nature, his having the genius to find some goodness in every fault. His manner of expression was generous: describing, for example, a piece of fruit as a pear once good gone rotten, rather than as a rotten pear. He was on the side of life; and because of his mindfulness in giving to others, others were able to respond to him.

Among artists, as Adler noted, discipline specific to the actor means working even if one doesn't feel like it. No matter what, in rehearsal and performance the actor has to act—without hesitation. She wanted us to get up onstage at the studio and practice our craft. She told us to "do your monkey act" or sing songs or do imitations at parties. Conversely, she did not want us going to auditions and setting ourselves up for judgment. We were to try out our stuff in supportive environments, but right away—not waiting until we felt secure.

> No actor ever feels he is forever good. Even when he works well and knows his work is good, he feels that tomorrow it will not be good. The actor has a built-in broken heart, which helps him to understand, but does not help him to win. There is no actor who looks like a banker at the end of his life. He looks distinguished, but he does not look as if he has won. The actor pays a price, and the price is his heart.

Adler expected us to offer our hearts to the work. The actor's discipline, she said, is to give one's self and keep one's humanity.

> Before all else, I am somebody who is trying to awaken in you what you have to a small proportion—your soul. I can only touch it. You must make

it aspire to something big. Don't expect too much help for that. I can only guide you a little bit. You have to struggle with making something out of this little thing in you. That is the historically basic work of man.

To wake up the soul is the essence of the actor's struggle for human development. If the actor keeps to the struggle, he will more than deserve the platform. He will symbolize its dignity.

The Principle is
DO NOT WITHDRAW FROM LIFE.

PHYSICAL STANDARDS

I am not the boss. I am here to help you be the boss over your muscles and everything.

Adler's mission for the first term included honing our tools to the standard correct for the actor, which meant making them suitable to express the epic ideas of modern drama. Calling the actor's body and voice his signature, she proposed that if the body and voice were normal, then the penmanship would be good. By normal she meant healthy, or having strength and flexibility that were sufficient to the task as well as being under control. By normal she did not mean a kind of speaking and moving that feels real or natural because it is one's habit, but speaking and moving that is real and natural because it meets the standards of the stage. Adler was advocating an aristocracy of the voice and body.

BODY

THE NORM: When she evaluated our physical condition, Adler's reaction was that she had to deal with "the last remnants of mankind." But what she needed in order to do her job effectively was people with tuned equipment. Indicating the existence in America of a pervasive lack of healthy habits in posture and appearance, she reproved us for chasing a trend of carelessness or sloppiness. Asking us not to be casual but to be severe with ourselves, she advised us to study with a movement teacher or somehow find the means to coordinate ourselves physically. She wanted our spines aligned and our heads held up, so we could sit, stand, and move normally.

> I cannot deal with broken material. Your homes
> have broken you. If I had walked or stood as you
> do, I would have gotten a black eye from my
> mother or father. But your way is apparently how
> you are allowed to stand at home. You had better fix
> it up for yourself. Fix your stance and your ability to
> be normal. I cannot start you unless you are mate-
> rial. I cannot build you if you have broken yourself,
> inside and out.

At the same time, Adler sympathized with America's
confusion about what constitutes a normal body. She said
that if we lived in Britain, for example, we could reflect the
standard of deportment set by the royalty, as do the British
preacher, parliamentarian, and actor. But here in America,
she regretted, "We have temporarily lost this kind of social
symbol. Ours is too broken, too individualistic. Any way
you want to walk or talk is the norm." Without any para-
gon of unbroken deportment, or at best with an image of
"anything goes," the American actor is left to find a normal
body for himself.

To guide us in our search for normal, Adler suggested we
look to cultures of the past to discover a physical aesthetic.
She particularly recommended the ancient Greeks, unified
through the disciplines of religion, theatre and athletics, as
a people who manifested in their sculpture the concept that
a natural body stretches upward, with an elevating energy.
This elevated body she considered the actor's norm, the
body the actor develops and the foundational body with
which the actor always begins to create a role. For characterization, for his profession in general, the actor simply

cannot afford an abnormal body, an unelevated, bent, cramped, or dehumanized body.

Another drawback for the actor raised in America, as identified by Adler, was inhibition. She blamed the Puritan ethic of restraint for a kind of minimal physical expression. She encouraged us to get rid of parochialism, because it creates rigidity in the body. The problem of the American actor, she said, is not an inability to act, but an inability to free his or her acting from the confines of a Puritanized body.

> You find yourself either ashamed of your body or defensive. It is not the case in Europe, where there is Lollobrigida. But here there is a lot of contraction, shame, pulling in, and making everything less than it is. It is a tradition of restriction, from which you need to free yourself.

Her aim was for us to dispense with smallness. We were to do every action fully, presenting ourselves unconstrained in life and finding our maximum capacity for gesture and movement onstage. The idea was that full physical expression allows the energy to thrive and the feelings to flow outward.

Adler asked us to consistently check ourselves against a sense of "I am the most perfect I can be," so that the actor's norm could become our norm. Essentially, we were to broaden our perspective, to appreciate ourselves as subjects aligned with Nature, rather than objects dictated to by society. This meant exercising our right to what Adler's mother had told her: "There is room for everybody on this earth. No one is taking up anybody else's place." By acknowledging our right to be on the earth, we could experience the support of the earth and move with confidence.

> No matter what else erodes, goes, or vanishes, except when you are buried beneath it the earth stays to hold you up. It is the same onstage. The platform will hold you up. No matter where you are—in the street, in the garden, onstage—the earth, because its nature is basic, will support you.

Experiencing the earth as solid allows the actor to experience standing, sitting, and walking as solid. Then he can extend any physical inclination to its maximum theatrical expression, without fear of faltering. The actor can trust that his base will not collapse or fail.

CONTROL: The next stage of our physical development was learning to apply control. Control meant using the minimum effort to produce and maintain a maximum physical effect. Adler explained that control depends on clarity, but not necessarily on comfort: "It is more important to be right than comfortable." Also, comfort to her did not imply relaxation but rather a kind of laxity or limpness. Control did imply relaxation, or a body not overcome by tension. General tension arises onstage because of a lack of control. It indicates an overexpenditure of energy because of ignorance of one's body or ignorance of what one needs to be doing in the moment onstage.

Adler agreed with Stanislavsky that, even though it may be argued that every actor tenses up somewhere in his body, a good actor does not let his tension spill over. A good actor is in touch with his tension and channels it to an appropriate place in his body. Otherwise, the actor finds himself in a state of general tension, which prohibits feeling anything and makes the acting mechanical.

She instructed us to use our energy properly, by first relaxing the whole body and then concentrating all our being on accomplishing whatever action was needed. We were not to worry about how much energy or muscle it takes to do an action. Simply, we were to do it, and in the doing we would discover the amount of energy or muscle it takes. Then we would know that this much—no more, no less—is what it takes.

Adler applied the same principle of doing only as much as is needed—no more, no less—to another function of control, which is to make a physical adjustment. A physical adjustment is some change or imperfection put into the body that demechanizes the acting and helps the actor relax. Having observed that "most acting is too ironed-out, too alike," Adler considered it artistically interesting to create something physically unusual.

As an example of a physical adjustment, she offered the case of two stiff fingers. To gain control of this physical adjustment, we were instructed to live with two stiff fingers in daily life, testing to see how we would play cards, dress, shop, eat, and shower with them. The point was to discover just how much muscle expenditure was necessary to maintain the two stiff fingers, without ever letting the adjustment consume us. At the same time, we could see that the adjustment affected to some degree everything we did. Adler warned against fictionalizing a physical adjustment by pretending, for example, that the two stiff fingers were the result of arthritis or an industrial accident. A physical adjustment is assimilated, made second nature, and kept under control with minimum effort. It is not acted, featured, or displayed. The only thing acted is the action, which may happen to be acted by a person with two stiff fingers.

Adler suggested the use of aids to help discover the minimal level of muscle needed to secure a physical adjustment. If someone wants to have heavy legs, for example, he can walk with iron in his shoes, until the sense of heaviness becomes his own. If an actor can live daily life with a physical adjustment, not letting the stiffness spill out of his two fingers or the heaviness out of his legs, then the actor can transfer the physical adjustment to the stage.

The technique, then, for making a physical adjustment is

- Locate the area you want to control.
- Decide how little muscle is needed to make and keep the control.
- Practice the control.
- Forget it.

Mastering the final step of forgetting a physical adjustment appreciably depends upon the next-to-final step of practicing it. Once the actor is able to forget it, the physical adjustment is free to produce spontaneity and individuality or idiosyncrasy in the acting. If the actor with two stiff fingers mixes himself a drink on stage, it is likely that some surprise—life!—will come into the mixing. Or if he goes to shake hands with the partner onstage, it is likely that their relationship will be enlivened. To the extent that a physical adjustment becomes second nature and is forgotten, the acting can become more real.

To validate this principle, Adler suggested observing people on the street. Every person can be seen as unique by virtue of some physical peculiarity, but no one generally goes around calling attention to his or her differences. Adler challenged us to recognize variety among human beings.

> Do you think people are all the same? They live with who they are. I know a man who has one good leg and a stump. Still, he walks to the bathroom and doesn't look at his limp. Another person is a hunchback. Another is a cripple. He has things on his mind other than his leg.

Physical idiosyncrasy helps reveal the humanity of a person. When idiosyncrasy is brought to the stage, it supports the actor's sense of reality.

Voice

THE NORM: Training the voice, according to Adler, involved defining the sound and speech qualities necessary to meet the demands of the stage. She noted:

- Any actor can talk and be heard on television, but a television actor cannot bring that voice to the stage.
- However the actor speaks to his grocer, it is not how he speaks on the platform.

Adler's first vocal requirement was sufficient volume. She was not so concerned with the particular quality of a voice, whether it was handsome, mellifluous or lilting, but she was adamant that it be heard in the front, back, and sides of the room:

> It is abnormal to use the voice without projection, because the nature of life is to stretch outward. A tree grows out, a bird calls out, a cow moos out, a hand is thrust out to say hello, and a person speaks out to reach another. It is insanity, madness, it makes no sense at all to talk in.

Her second vocal requirement was that sounds be properly enunciated and effectively employed. Having acknowledged that human speech has many aspects more troublesome than the call of a bird or the moo of a cow, Adler invited us to stimulate our voices by becoming familiar with the complexities and nuances of language. Considering that standard American speech and vocabulary might be alien to us, she noted that without them our range would be severely limited and our expression hampered. "It is not good," she said, "for the actor to do Shakespeare through clenched teeth." To articulately convey the scope of classical and modern drama, the actor needs to grow friendly with words. He has to learn to respect the specific natures of words, so as to communicate the meanings behind words. If the actor does not enlarge his understanding of language and use of sound, "He is unfit to talk, much less to act," Adler contended.

CONTROL: Once we had trained our vocal instrument to meet the standard of the platform, we could, according to Adler, "monkey with it in a thousand ways." She had us try various speech impediments. Working on a lisp, for example, we located and learned to control the necessary muscles. We checked to see if we could remain ourselves, simply and unaffectedly, without exhibiting or performing, without falling into a characterization, while speaking with a lisp. We discovered that all one needs for a lisp is to adjust the tongue, placing it against the upper teeth instead of the lower, when sounding an *s*. Nothing else is needed: no other muscle adjustments, no pushing out the words, no raising the vocal pitch, no acting cute or behaving like a child or an idiot, and no being concerned with anything, least of all with the lisp, other than with what we were communicating. Adler explained that, like everyone else, "The person who lisps also gets sick, is in great pain, and goes to the doctor, too, except that he says, 'I can't thtand it!'" In other words, she made it clear once and for all that even though someone speaks with an impediment, he knows what he is talking about.

In the realm of accents and dialects, also governed by the technique of making a physical adjustment, Adler again opted for simplicity. We were taught to change just enough of our pronunciation to produce the sense of an accent, not to revamp our entire speech. For example, by placing the *r* sound far back in the throat and rolling it as if gargling, we could produce one aspect of a simple French accent. With this *r* sound and, at most, two other French sounds, and with nothing else belonging to the French, we could create an illusion of something French. But since we were not French, we were not to attempt to control the entire culture. What we were to control was our speech, selectively.

Our homework was to listen to impediments, accents, and dialects in life.

Find a southerner with whom you can sit and talk. You can steal something from his speech, but don't take the whole south. If you do, yah'll gohnna dreep sooo mehnee magnoleeah blahsuums, yah'll jes gohnna keell evreebahdee.

Adler also suggested we consult books on accents and dialects to learn how to write out the accent or dialect of a role phonetically and study from that.

Whatever vocal adjustment the actor steals from life or art, it must be made his or her own—not an imitation, not an improvisation, and not a ready-made cliché. As long as the actor's only muscular involvement is with the control of a few selected sounds, there is no danger of his speech slipping into a conventional pattern or rythm. For example, a southern dialect does not have to be slow. A vocal adjustment requires only the rythm of the actor's norm.

The hallmark, then, of a vocal adjustment is simplicity, evoking a sense of authenticity and not artificaility. With this in mind, Adler remarked upon the seasoned experience of John Gielgud.

In a magazine article, Gielgud said not to embroider but to cut down. Also, he said that the acting becomes better after you've played for six weeks and done the cutting. He's right, except that you must cut down now, even if he does it after six weeks. You see, the English embroider everything. "What a lahvely dhaay." An actor must first look at the day before speaking about it. But over there, it all tends to be ready-made. The English have forgotten the contact with the day, "reahlly."

Mastering a simple speech adjustment takes the actor

out of fear and puts him into control of the text. The only justifiable fear, according to Adler, was that of a child, in that the child has no control over himself. An indispensable step for the actor in transcending fear is taking control of his body and voice.

The Principle is
DO NOT DO MORE OR LESS
THAN THE ACTOR'S NORM.

CHAPTER II

The Resources of the Actor

The other segment of training during the first term at the Stella Adler Conservatory, concurrent with cultivating one-self, was the cultivation of an actor's approach to life. This entailed heightening our appreciation and use of the world around us. We were expected to perceive everything in a new way, to open up our imagination to limitless possibilities, to acquire a taste for big ideas, and to learn to handle material things properly. By delving into the life of the world, we were to build up a wealth of understanding upon which to draw for creation. Adler warned us against thinking we could rely only on speaking the words of a playwright. She wanted us to be as full of life and ideas as was the playwright when writing the words he or she wrote for actors to speak. Our process of enrichment, then, required observing the natures of people, places, and things—and collecting these natures—in order to reflect them back to the world from the stage.

THE LIFE OF THE WORLD

Nature is most of all to be studied.

It was Adler's custom to start class with a story or description of some person or incident she had noticed on her way to the studio. She taught us to look out for whatever showed up in the world around us, and to remember it. Observation was a nurturing activity to feed the imagination and enrich the mind. In fact, in Adler's opinion, seeing was the key to acting.

In particular, we were to look for the nature within whatever we saw. Since the nature of something—its essence and way of working— never varies but remains constant, it can be discovered through observation. The natures we found became our working material, taken from life and transferred to the stage. Even though the stage (fictitious) is different from life (real), the actor is faithful to the fundamental nature of anything represented onstage.

In the world, of course, everything is taken for granted as having a life and a nature all its own. But onstage, the actor must impart to everything a life logical to its nature. This creation of life is rooted in the practice of seeing, which was to Adler a spiritual activity. She said, "In a godless culture, an art form can save you. You can believe in what you create."

Having declared that an artistic life is sustained by observation, Adler cited the habits of creative people.

> In his letters, Thomas Wolfe wrote, "This week I'm looking at noses." That's good. It's good to see that some noses droop down like waterfalls. There are writers and artists from all over the world who go to see the trees in season in the south of France.

Likewise, our job was to look and to see. Adler encouraged us, for example, to discern different ways of walking: the parading on Fifth Avenue, the slouching on Ninth, the reticent walk in Chinatown, or the shuffle in Harlem. Observation would lead us to locate physically in ourselves a particular way of walking different from our own. Also, by looking into various neighborhoods, we could see how a particular environment demanded particular behavior. We discovered that the life around us was a grand resource, or, as Adler put it, "The role exists in the world, not in the actor."

In addition to observing contemporary life, we were to research historical life, especially for classical roles. Having acknowledged that modern Americans are generally denied a firsthand view of emperors, queens, and statespersons as well as castles, temples, and battlefields, Adler discouraged us from decrying our own situation. We were not to moan, "All I see is my father who plays poker every night, so how can I play Julius Caesar?" We were to recognize that history was on display for us to examine in museums and books, and that we could immerse ourselves in the art and relics of past cultures.

When seeing, we were to exercise good judgment, learning to distinguish between the epic and the trivial things of life. The epic, those things that have gone on and will go on eternally, Adler distinguished as a boy tossing a ball, a mother feeding her baby, wind blowing through pine trees, and war being waged and peace cultivated. These timeless phenomena, which vibrate with a universal rhythm, served to bring our focus away from the busy-ness of daily life by inviting us to share in a sense of eternity. By measuring up to the eternal universal, the actor brings a dramatic approach to the events and ideas occurring in plays.

The actor also exercises good judgment in deciding what is beautiful and what is ugly among what he sees. In this way, he can discover how he feels about things. Adler suggested that we initially gravitate toward observing things we like, things that catch our heart immediately. But to really like something, she pointed out, means to have seen and known it clearly and specifically, according to its nature and true function. She said that when a person really likes something in the sense that he has caught its particular nature, then he responds to it. Adler illustrated how people do or do not respond to things, depending upon how they see them.

> Sometimes, when a husband and wife go on a trip together, he says, "My God! Do you know what that is? Why, that's Notre Dame!" And she replies, "Yes, I know. I can see it." They are each seeing in Notre Dame something entirely different.

Adler outlined three ways of seeing. The first and most common, almost exclusively concerned with the facts of a thing, she called *Banking*.

> If I ask someone, "What do you have there?" and he, who is holding a handful of banknotes, replies, "Five, ten, fifteen, twenty, thirty—yes, I have thirty dollars in cash." And if describing what he saw at the grocery he says, "I saw some grapes, and pears, and bananas," then he makes a good banker but not a good actor. He sees things in the manner of accounting.

The Banking way of seeing takes note of the facts; for example, "It's a rose and it's red. It has a two-inch stem and four petals." This way, Adler explained, is unhealthy for the actor, since the more the rose is described factually, the less it is a rose. In other words, the moment an object is given a bank account, it begins to die.

With the second way, *Seeing the Life*, the viewer lets the object speak to him or her.

> If, again, with the banknotes, he says, "I have some bills here that are rather dirty. Perhaps we can get them changed. Oh! Here's a two-dollar bill. Is that worth anything?" Or if with the fruit, he says, "I saw some fantastic pears that were big, but looked too expensive to buy. Then I saw those wonderful Malaga grapes, long and very sweet. There were also some of those great big blue grapes, and the baby ones, the little green ones. Those you can eat by the pound, and, by the way they're very cheap!"—that is more the actor's way.

Seeing the Life, which is heightened seeing, respects the object's nature, acknowledging that it has a life of its own. Also, it gives birth to a relationship between the viewer and the object, whereby some form of communication arises between them. When the actor looks into an object's nature, lets it be, and listens to its story, he is fed by the object's life.

The third way of seeing, *Traveling*, is the optimum way for the actor. It occurs when the viewer not only lets the object live, but also allows it to lead him wherever it may go. Picking up a pair of spectacles, Adler demonstrated.

> Well, these are mostly glass. I suppose a lot of people

wear them, but they're really rather ugly, just two pieces of glass. They're not meant for anything but to see through. I used to wear glasses, but I've given them up. I guess I sacrifice [my vision] because glass per se has no pleasantness in it. Wouldn't you feel much better if there were wine in the glass, or whiskey? But by itself, this piece of glass has no personality. The rim around it is kind of opaque. Do you know stones that are opaque? They are the colors of death, the pale greens. But this is almost a kind of brown, and it's plastic. It's nice when it's amber, like amber earrings. They change color. People don't wear amber anymore, except in Paris, where the shops are full of it. I guess that's because it's very hard for the French to give up anything they've had in the past.

With the Traveling way of seeing, the power of the object arouses in the viewer his or her recollection of things he or she may never have consciously considered but that lie somewhere within his memory. Guesswork or supposition does not enter into Traveling. With the object as catalyst for a chain of references, the viewer goes and keeps on going, traveling as if he could go on forever—discovering, uncovering, recovering what he holds within. By practicing this way of seeing, we came to trust Adler's axiom that "every object contains one's whole life." She wanted to awaken our sense of already knowing and having all there is to know and have.

Having contended that "the actor is drawn to art because he cannot elsewhere express very much of what he has inside him," she asked us to expand our internal life.

The actor is like a writer, full of impressions that speak to him. He does not go around being a sort of clerk without a job, saying, "I'll have bacon and eggs." When he gets bacon and eggs, he sees them, as well as the waitress, the table, and the restaurant with its rushed activity. He gathers in the place. He is able to see that the floor has dirt on it but the table is spotless, the coffee is weak, nobody is really paying any attention to each other, and everybody is in a hurry. He takes in. He is not there just to eat, pay his check, and go out. He is able to live there—watching, seeing, and understanding by saying, "What is it? What am I looking at?"—the way a painter does, the way a writer does.

Adler's theory was that when things are respectfully seen, when they are neither emptied of nor deprived of their lives, they resuscitate the viewer. Respectful viewing evokes a two-way flow of sympathy, or a functioning of love. Adler said, "The more capacity the actor has to understand the nature of things, the more compassionate he will be."

This resource of seeing also functions for the actor in listening. Adler explained that to listen is to see what someone else is saying, to follow the picture, to take in and not blot out another's verbalized vision. To listen is to be as vibrantly alive with images of what one is hearing as is the partner speaking. It is to be active, not passive. It is not to wait for pauses, stops, or punctuation before responding.

Adler said we should never find ourselves sitting without seeing. We could travel anyplace at anytime, following the nature within the simplest object. Our trips were not to be logical but creative. We were to expand our sight, building things, growing things, until realizing that we could, as Adler said, "write volumes" on what we were able to see. By means of observation, the actor makes of the world an abundant resource.

The Principle is
BE FULL OF THE LIFE AROUND YOU.

THE LIFE OF THE IMAGINATION

All life in art is Imaginative.

According to Adler, the source of acting is the imagination, and the value of the actor's contribution depends upon use of imagination. She said that the imagination embraces "everything that you know consciously, and at least ten billion times more that you know unconsciously." Tapping the unconscious, which she called "the life within," provokes the actor to act. Basically, the actor uses conscious knowledge to awaken unconscious knowledge on which to draw.

The actor's imagination functions in various ways. Overall, it serves as a filter through which the fiction of the stage is passed in order to make it real. The imagination is the actor's solution to his stickiest problem: how do I avoid speaking words or saying lines that I neither believe nor feel? The actor uses his imagination to give life to each element about which he must speak—any idea, event, person, or thing found in the text. The actor can build a world behind and under the words of the script, thus sharing, as Adler said, "in the miracle of life." She emphasized that mere facts are not what is presented to an audience; rather, a creation is presented.

Adler exhorted us to free our sight from our own habitual circumstances, including our own culture, home, neighborhood, and family. With the eyes of imagination, we were to envision fresh territory, seeing ourselves active in uncustomary situations. Actual life tends toward redundancy, but imagined life transports us to other times, other places, in company with other people. Adler suggested how much more interesting it would be to imagine preparing coffee in her kitchen using her coffee pot, than routinely making coffee in our own situation. She advised us to train our imagination to see things clearly and in detail. The idea was that the more specifically the actor sees, the more he is propelled into exploring his own unconscious life.

She argued against speculating whether what we imagined actually existed or not. Whatever the imagination engenders has a right to exist and does. When Adler asked us to imagine a lemon tree, she believed us capable of growing some kind of lemon tree, whether or not we had actually ever seen one. As long as a lemon tree remained alive in our imagination, it existed and could be brought to the stage.

To train our mind's eye, Adler narrated the outlines of a scene. She asked us to wend our way along a country road. As soon as we heard "country road," we were expected to recognize immediately that we had been placed—put into circumstances—and that we would have to visualize the circumstances in detail. When the actor sees specifically, he knows the place where he is. From knowing where he is, he can figure out what needs to be done there. Also, by seeing specifically, the actor is protected from speaking of unknown places or circumstances. Adler explained:

> The playwright is never going to give you a country road that belongs to you. He will only give you to say, "I was walking along a country road." You will supply the body, saying, "It's dusty, the color of rust streaming through cornfields, high on both sides." Though the playwright indicates the circumstances, he does not give them to the actor.

In other words, the imagination lets the actor know what he is talking about.

For the actor to know what he is talking about, Adler explained, means to understand the logic of the place and the nature of everything in it. She called this "managing the circumstances," the importance of which she illustrated.

> Suppose onstage I say to you, "Would you like to have a drink?" and your answer is, "No thanks, I have one." If we were in the Peruvian mountains, you wouldn't know what the hell kind of drink you were talking about. It could be fermented llama milk. Or if you pick up your tumbler in a Shakespeare play and say, "Health to the King," and if you don't know what you are drinking, then you are drinking the words.

The actor manages the circumstances by assimilating the logic of where he is. He figures out what kind of drink that place has to offer, as well as the nature of everything else coming his way.

So, the actor's goal via the imagination is to bring to life and to personalize every element given by the playwright. The actor must make the play his own. The actor must not let the play remain the printed words of a playwright's text. "If it is Shakespeare's," Adler said, "throw it out. It has to be yours." To dispel any mystery about how the actor personalizes the facts of a script, Adler explained that it is simply a natural process of slowly opening up in order to give birth. The actor begins to appropriate a section of the text by asking questions.

- What am I saying?
- Can I say this in my own words?
- Can I put them into a place?
- What place is it?
- What is necessary for this place?
- What must be done in this place?

Such questions impel the actor to think, see, and select, and finally to imagine himself doing something somewhere. The more the actor personalizes his images, the more he can knowledgeably and honestly speak onstage—from personal imagined experience. Personalization lets the actor access his unconscious life, getting his feelings to flow.

Adler also recommended the imagination for arousing sympathy for a character. The technique was to devise a story in which we would see the character doing something in a place, so as to care about the character. For example, she asked us to imagine what happens to a man holding a large package while waiting for the bus. To be able to care about the man, it was essential to imagine something like: "When the bus stopped, the man tried to board it, but the package was so big and there were so many people on the bus, that he just decided to get down, turn around, and walk home." On the contrary, it would not have been helpful merely to say, "The man didn't take the bus." The former, which is seeing the life behind a fact, lets the actor feel the insides of another's shoes. The latter, which is stating the fact, leaves the actor with cold feet.

Using the imagination to give life to facts is "a big secret of acting," Adler said. She in fact credited imagination with nine-tenths of the acting. Imagination makes the actor's work honest. Without the use of imagination, words are just words, the place is no place, the objects are nothing, the characters are nobodies, and the actor is empty, his acting a fabrication. With imagination, words have meaning, places and objects have reality, bodies have character, and the actor is replete with images and feelings, giving him the impetus to do something. With imagination, the acting proceeds from a source.

The Principle is
EVERYTHING ON STAGE IS A LIE
UNTIL YOU MAKE IT TRUTHFUL.

THE LIFE OF IDEAS

Nine-tenths of the attraction of acting is a love affair with ideas. A small part is money, fame, or something like that.

Adler encouraged us to expand our perspective. She wanted us to understand the "big ideas" of the collective human consciousness, and to raise our responses to these ideas above street-level glibness. This mental stretching, in her opinion, was essential to actor training.

> Just as the good writer gets dissatisfied producing mystery novels, so does the good actor need more than light comedy. The actor needs big ideas. His size comes from his ability to understand the problems of our time, which he carries in his core. Understanding is the center of his being.

Adler held that, even if the purpose of theatre is to entertain, the modern theatre, beginning with Ibsen, is not a theatre of jokes but of moral ideas relevant to human society. The modern playwright has an ethical aim. The modern play abounds in big (immutable) ideas pertaining to humanity, as opposed to little (relative) ideas pertaining to a limited sector.

The big ideas of a drama support and propel its theme. In Adler's description, the typically modern theme has to do with a loss of identity or the demeaning of humanity, because of our modern lifestyle. She said the context for this modern theme may be a loss of tradition, including belief in God; a loss of community, including an ethical order; or a loss of family life, including honor. The loss theme would generally be dramatized through a life-or-death situation, with the threatened life most likely being the life of the soul—as is the case of Willy Loman in Arthur Miller's *Death of a Salesman*, Miss Alma in Tennessee Williams's *Summer and Smoke*, Joe Bonaparte in Clifford Odets's *Golden Boy*, or Jamie in Eugene O'Neill's *Long Day's Journey into Night*.

Adler characterized modern drama as conveying "the dilemma of people stranded in a world in which nobody wins, nobody loses, and there is no solution." Accordingly, she saw the modern character as subject to arbitrary fortune or fate. He is no longer subject to the Greek gods, the European king, or the One True Church. He is bereft of religious guidance and traditional rules. He is left with only himself to scavenge for a personal morality. His end may be either fortunate or unfortunate, but cannot be judged either right or wrong. To emphasize the stakes of modern drama, Adler heralded it as larger than Shakespeare: "Hamlet is interested in Denmark, but the modern character is interested in humanity."

The actor fits into the scheme of dramatizing modern ideas by aligning with the playwright. Adler said that the playwright is able to assert a morality upon the play because he or she understands humanity's loss of faith in modern life. In fact, the playwright has suffered for his or her understanding. The actor, in turn, must understand our moral loss—which causes him to suffer, the price he pays for the privilege of ascending the platform.

The modern actor bears the responsibility of grasping the moral questions of our day. He needs clarity of mind and hard-earned values. Adler considered it detrimental for the actor to accommodate or appropriate what she called "audience" (common) thinking or "audience" (conventional) standards. Rather, the actor imperatively engages in thinking that is as complex as the eminent ideas of modern drama. The actor's vocation—"to interpret the author's ideas so that the audience might be aroused to an understanding of their own lives"—necessarily puts him in the position of public illuminator or public servant, but not in the position of the public. Yet the actor does not patronize the audience. The ideas of a play, after all, though promulgated by the playwright and articulated by the actor, belong to (and stem from) the lives of everyone.

Adler explained that the ideas of a play could be contrary to the actor's personal beliefs. Even so, the play's moral framework, not his own, is the actor's concern. Having pointed out that there is "no play written about my life and my facts," Adler guided us toward the actor's path: to have an "ongoing aim to serve, to give, and to sacrifice something along the way." Walking this path enables the actor to expand his own consciousness and that of the audience.

Our work was to search out big ideas and fall in love with them. Our work was not to memorize the lines of a play. Memorizing lines causes the actor to lose sight of a play's moral framework. Learning and speaking the lines is the final step in the actor's work, just as writing the dialogue was the end product of the playwright's work. Adler told the story of an actress who, wanting help with a role, asked if Stella would read the lines for her. Adler answered, "Yes, certainly, but why? Don't you believe that I can read English?"

The actor has no business counting lines and practicing line readings. It is not the actor's job to reiterate English, but to deliver his understanding of the ideas of a play, revealing their excitement, color, and power. As Adler noted, "The difference between a good actor and a student playing Hamlet is that the actor has made the ideas his own, while the student speaks English." Having asked us to select an excerpt from an essay by Emerson or another writer who articulates big ideas, Adler outlined a technique for making ideas one's own:

- Understand within you what the author is talking about. Consult a dictionary for any word that has uncertainty for you. Use a thesaurus to find synonyms that stimulate you emotionally.
- Write out the essay in your own words.
- Return to the author's text, and read it in sequences of thought. Do not memorize the words.
- Study the sequences, finding the point of attention in each, so as not to wander. Find the overall growth of the progression of sequences, either upward or downward. Learn the progression of the sequences until it's second nature.
- Using your own words, tell the sequences to someone, getting him or her to understand you. Keep to the point of each sequence, and get the overall growth.
- Return to the text. Using the author's words, tell the sequences to someone, getting him or her to understand you. Fill the words with their full meanings, as you've understood them.

This sequence technique precludes becoming casual with words and taking them at face value. By not memorizing the words, the actor is freed to get a feel for the language. He particularizes or individualizes words with the sense and personality he perceives behind them and under them. It is a process of shaping and coloring that results in words not sounding either all the same or even neutral. Adler said that the key to particularization is imagination. To enable the audience to perceive what he is talking about, the actor first sees it in his own imagination.

Sometimes the language does not need coloring but to be put into perspective, as is the case with lines that are there to convey information, for example, lines announcing the play's time and place or a character's background. Informational language, including exposition, resides atmospherically in the middle, between the emotional levels of light and dark. Other language, however, especially words that stand as signposts for the expression of big ideas, need a considered and considerable response. Adler explained, for example, that words like peace, war, struggle, love, death, children, humanity, hope, truth, charity, are not colloquial and do not convey information. They do not reside in a middle atmosphere, and the sequence in which they live cannot be treated informally. She referred us to Shakespeare, Shaw, Ibsen, Strindberg, and more recent social dramatists in order to find signpost words and the big ideas they announce. Big ideas, she noted, are expressed in classical plays with an abundance of words, disclosing the playwright's command of language. In modern plays, however, big ideas are written with fewer words and more prosaically. Still, the actor needs the same commitment of energy to impart the big ideas of modern drama as he needs to communicate the humanistic poetry of Shakespeare or the intellectual dynamism of Shaw. Thus, Adler contended, "Realism is not about getting up on stage. It is also not the style of acting to the minimum.

Realism is about acting a theme propelled by big ideas."
She admonished us to act to the maximum.

Acting to the maximum implies being full of the love
derived from understanding big ideas. Adler offered a technique for acting a theme:

- Think deeply about the big ideas found in an essay or
  monologue.
- Get each sequence inside yourself.
- Have the determination to reach someone with the big
  ideas.

The power to project the magnitude of a big idea comes
from two aspects of the physical training:

- The vocal energy to extend beyond the level of everyday conversation.
- The physical capacity to align the body to suit the content of the idea.

When the actor's voice and body are correctly defined, the
audience is moved to pay attention to the content of a big
idea. In illustrating the correct physical form for the expression of a big idea, Adler first described what it is not:

> If I have to say, "A girlfriend of mine told me that
> the best way to get a maid is to read the *New York
> Times* ad section," it is possible, because of the
> nature of that statement, for me to sit down lei-
> surely and even remove my shoes. It is possible to
> break [collapse] the posture while delivering that
> thought. When the English is not selected, then

neither the body nor the voice needs selection. The form is loose.

But when the idea is sizeable and the language is not collo-quial, a physical adjustment is in order.

A big idea needs platform, a presence. It needs from you a voice. You cannot have a crumpled tie and a banana in your hand. You cannot sit and be comfortable, but must be set in some place, located. You must be in the form.

The physical form for the expression of big ideas is a body worthy of sculpture and a voice worthy of recording.

When a character conveys a big idea, he or she may be exploring its meaning, experiencing its magnitude, or clar-ifying it, explaining it, and using it to educate someone. With whatever form of expression the character articulates a big idea, the actor thinks the idea through while speak-ing it, as if for the first time. The actor gives birth to the idea, discovering it as he goes, coming to terms with the idea in the presence of the stage partner and the audience, as though they were all together in discussion. The actor must achieve the psychic size demanded of the acting profession, which ultimately makes the idea, the dramatic struggle, and himself more human onstage. To act a theme truthfully, Adler said, "The acting must be done as a human being fighting for some values. If it is done as an actor, the technique is weak."

The Principle is
UNDERSTAND, DO NOT LIE.

THE LIFE OF MATERIALS

The play comes nine-tenths from the outside, including from the ability to be at home in the costume.

Adler was against attempting to approach a role by looking for it inside oneself. The effort to bring one's insides out usually resulted in a mishmash of what she called "emotional kvetching"—faked feelings—and lies, resulting in a frightened performer. Having asked us, "Who said, 'If crying was all that was needed in acting, the greatest actress would be my grandmother'?" She pulled us outside ourselves, toward the life of materials.

COSTUME

Costume is a viable avenue to the inside self. It provokes a response. It compels the actor to move, walk, and sit in a manner different from his habit, in the manner appropriate to the costume. Adler extolled the value of the costume.

> You think that costume is Brooks Brothers. But the costume is a whole creative point of identification for the actor with its nature—its quality, texture, the way it hangs, and the reason for its being as it is. Costume is more creative than the emotion, much more than the words.

To wear and use the costume as the costume demanded, according to what Adler called its "norm," was to own it. Our goal was to discover the costume's nature and understand what that nature represented. Then we could apply our understanding of the costume (an outside element) to understanding the psychology (inside) of the character wearing the costume.

Adler proposed that the actor contribute to the look of the costume rather than meekly accept someone else's design. In support, she related a story.

> When I was eight years old, my father said to me, "Well, you're going to play young Spinoza. Now, I would like you to go to the library and get some pictures of Spinoza and then go to the costume designer and tell him what kind of costume you need." Why did he say that? He said it because he believed that an actor is responsible, whatever age he may be. He was talking to a young actress. He was not talking to his child. He didn't have any children. He had actors.

Adler taught us to understand the costume first of all from the point of view of the character's social class. She said that even though in modern society a person's social standing may not always be visible in his everyday apparel, onstage the costume must clearly reveal the character's social class. Class demarcation grounds the actor, enabling him to know where his character came from and what behavior he or she ought to exhibit—based on what the character is wearing.

Adler challenged us to experiment with costume, in order to experience the impact of it on our conduct and feelings.

> In the Comédie-Française, the actors all come into rehearsal in very formal, old-fashioned clothes to

give them a sense of being in the theatre. They
practice for hours and hours the behavior in accordance with the clothes. In the old days of theatre in
America, the actors wore clothes [in daily life] that
made them feel important. But you wear clothes
that make you feel unimportant. If you want to put
a man onstage and give him a real sense of defeat,
let him wear your shirt. But put him in an officer's
uniform, with a sword, and he will never sit around
the way you do.

The effect of the costume derives from the costume's
particular nature, which the actor allows to speak to him
rather than he to it. The actor discovers the nature of each
element of costume, finding out how to treat it, handle it,
and wear it, so as not to deny its life. Adler used the example of a top hat.

Find out its nature. Where does it live? It lives in a
box, which gives you information about it. It has
a certain value because it lives in a box that is tied
with a ribbon. When you have a hat that is housed
in a box, you know it needs a certain kind of care.

She cautioned us not to impose an artificial or generic
nature upon something whose specific nature was yet
unknown to us. Basically, she said, "Do not put something
on unless you know how to take it off." The actor understands the costume before wearing it. Otherwise, he or she
is wearing a lie.

Have you seen people in the movies dressed as

Christian soldiers, walking around all slumped over?
You see that a lot in the opera. They are wearing
the costume, but don't know its life, or what to
do with it. They don't know how to put it down,
where it should be put down, how to pick it up,
how to clean it.

The costume is approached as a stranger until its
nature—what is logically true about it—reveals itself. It
is approached tentatively, cautiously, respectfully. To get
acquainted with the costume, the actor makes himself available to it. This approach is especially crucial, Adler insisted,
when trying any element of costume from another period
of history. Period things cannot at all be used like things
from modern times. A cape cannot be worn as a coat; don-
ning a cape, we discovered, requires one clean sweep rather
than three untidy jerks.

Adler taught that, since period clothing is virtually
unknown in modern culture, we needed to understand
period costume in light of the society for which it was
designed. The cape, because it has a certain volume and
flow, told us it was invented to offer the wearer a status,
an appearance, and a relationship to himself and his society
that is different from the experience of a person wearing a
coat. Likewise, the actor is unfamiliar with the social behavior of a period character. To portray a king, for example,
the actor might become familiar with being ceremoniously
assisted down steps and carried through streets. The actor
might need to get used to wearing a crown and perhaps a
cape, so that these do not hinder him and he is able to use
them normally. Adler guided us toward a normal use of the
costume.

All the crown requires is for you to wear it. It does not require you to squint your eyes or stiffen your shoulders. Its nature does not allow you to bob up and down when you walk with it on. Therefore, you are actually protected by the life of the crown. Though you are in another culture, if you have understood the norm of that period and class, you will not distort the nature of the costume.

Because the actor respects the nature of the costume, he can work with it creatively rather than according to some stage convention. The actor personalizes the use of the costume, thereby personalizing his acting. Adler noted that once we had discovered the cape's nature and its norm of use, then we could fly with it, or cover something with it, or run with somebody under it. "The cape must belong to the actor," Adler said, "not to Eaves Costumes." Ultimately, the actor does not so much wear the costume as own the costume.

Whether a crown or an old sweater, each element of the costume takes the actor one step toward becoming the character. When we lent our bodies to an old sweater with sagging pockets, our bodies discovered the behavior suitable to an old sweater. Because of this power of the costume to effect practical results, Adler esteemed the costume as the actor's most reliable starting point for creating a role.

You don't need the Method to put on a sweater. The Method is to help you when you're in trouble. At times, you cannot or need not use it at all. What you can use, and always need, is the norm of the costume. Get it and don't suffer it.

"Don't suffer it" meant to know and effortlessly follow the costume's nature. When the actor knows the cape, when he and the cape are no longer strangers, then the actor does not need to fuss with the cape.

Adler reminded us that the material of theatrical costume is not necessarily of the same quality, texture, weave, and construction as its real-life counterpart. Consequently, she considered it all the more necessary to treat each element of costume according to the nature of what it represents—as if it were real-life apparel.

> In the theatre, you will be given a metal crown. But when you have to take it off, do not take off a metal crown. Know that it is gold and has weight. The weight will help you take it off. You control the weight, whether the crown is actually made of metal or paper.

When the actor treats the costume according to its norm, he is in control of the costume. In Adler's opinion, because the actor is in control of an old sweater, a cape, a little kerchief from Russia, or Queen Elizabeth's crown, the character can enter into him. She asserted, in fact, that the costume has the capacity to give the actor "the whole play."

PROPERTIES

Every prop has its own nature—wide, large, narrow, small, heavy, rough, sweet—which must not be overlooked or dismissed. As Adler noted, a prop's nature must be known and respected.

> If I say I am going to take a drink of milk, and

then stick the cup to my nose, there would be
something insane about that. I have to drink with
my mouth. I must obey the nature of the cup, the
milk, and drinking.

In the case of confronting an unfamiliar object, Adler
said to study it until we understood its nature. We discovered, for example, that the nature of writing with a quill is
different from writing with a ballpoint pen. Adler explained
that a period or unfamiliar object could not be used in a
contemporary or familiar way.

If I give a wallet to you, you know how to use it. If
I give a wallet to a monkey, he doesn't know how to
use it. If I give a sword to you, you don't know how
to use it, because it's a foreigner to you and you to
it. You must become a friend to it.

The way to befriend an object, according to Adler, was to
pay attention to it. When confronted with a scroll, it was
the scroll that told us the way to open and read it.

The prop not only tells the actor what to do with it
but also helps reveal the character. A cane, for example,
as opposed to a gnarled stick, discloses the social class to
which the character belongs, as does a fan, a lorgnette,
a wig, or a crown. Adler stressed that the props must be
selected by the actor—because it is the actor's responsibility
to reveal the character—and not be left solely to the discre-
tion of the properties person. The actor bases his selection
of a prop on his capacity to respond to it. Once a prop has
been selected, the actor deepens his connection with it by

giving it an imaginative history. As Adler explained, the history of a prop includes details, such as

- How it looked when it was first made or purchased.
- How it has changed since coming into the character's possession.

Building a history for a prop gives it an identity and enables the actor to relate to it personally.

Also by means of imagination, the actor determines the current condition of a prop. For example, we imagined our prop pen as having a crooked point or being out of ink. Adler suggested not confining a prop to some banal life-lessness, but giving it an imagined personality—a theatrical reality logical to the prop's nature. For example, we imagined a black table to be a burnt table. Through imagination, the actor develops a relationship with the prop, letting him feel something about it when using it.

When the actor gives a prop a history and a current condition, it ceases to be a prop and becomes a living object. In keeping with her advice never to take anything onstage for granted, Adler remarked that just as there is no costume—there are clothes—there are no props—there are personal belongings.

The Principle is
DISCOVER ITS NATURE.

CHAPTER III

Action: What the Actor Does

In the second term of training at the Stella Adler Conservatory, we began to act. This is not to say that during the first term we had never done an action. We had, but on the simplest physical level, neither complicated nor psychological. Doing actions—including studying their natures, the circumstances around them, the attitude of the doer, and the justification for doing them—was the concern of the second term.

THE PHYSIOLOGY OF ACTION

The field of acting is not talking things over. They [theatre people] say, "It's in three acts and twelve scenes and things happen."

To emphasize the danger of approaching acting through the words of a text, Adler exclaimed: "We are up against the word!" and "Words are empty!" and "Words need filling!" The language of theatre is not the words on a page. The actor cannot take the words of a text literally as printed, since words often mean other than what they appear to mean. "Oh, come on," as Adler pointed out, does not necessarily mean "Come along with me." The language of theatre is what results from the life behind and under the words. Adler called this living language the "doable nature" of words.

Every group of words, phrases, or sentences that makes up a sequence of thought has behind it some able-to-be-physicalized intention. This physicalizable intention Adler called "the action." She defined the action as "what I am doing most which involves where I am doing it." So, the actor's language is action—the result of the life behind and under the words.

Since an action has to do with potency—with some objective to be accomplished—the actor states the action in the infinitive form of the verb. To Study is an action. Adler advised us to state our action with the verb that most moved us. To Study, for example, may be more movingly expressed as To Acquire or To Imbibe or To Pursue. The actor uses terminology that motivates him to do something. Beyond identifying the action of a sequence, the actor must need the action—the need thus inciting the doing.

Adler taught that if we came upon a seemingly undoable action, because of its being too general, we could break it down into doable parts. To Work in the Garden, which is general, becomes viable when broken down into doable chores; for example, To Rake the Leaves and To Trim the Hedge. The action should be stated as something possible to do.

Altogether, the actions found in a script form the skeleton, the barest outline, of the play. They form a recipe and not the banquet. The actor's job, by means of imagination, tools, and resources, is to put flesh on the bones or food on the table.

Each character in a play pursues a main action or aim (or, in Stanislavsky's terminology, a super-objective), which is what the character is trying to accomplish most in the course of his dramatized life. All his subsidiary actions feed this main aim. As Adler explained, the goal of acting is to do truthfully, moment by moment, step by step, each successive action in a given place. Adler said, "Acting is telling the truth that is there for you. It is not pretending."

Knowing the nature of an action is to know what to do but not how to do it. Adler warned against planning the how of an action. Deciding in advance how an action should be done leads to what she called "following" the action, which is a kind of harassment. Planning the how imprisons imagination and precludes spontaneity.

> An action is what you do most, but it never includes in what manner you do it. If my small physical action is To Button My Coat, I do not say that I'll grasp the material with the right hand, take the button with the left, approach the buttonhole, gently sliding the button into the opening, and give a left-handed twist until it passes through. I simply button my coat. Just do your action.

Not planning the how is what keeps the action fresh and always as if being done for the first time. Not planning the how keeps the acting alive.

Since the actor is constantly being asked by the playwright, director, and himself to do things, Adler said that the actor's ensuing responsibility is to be in charge of what he is doing. This means to understand the natures of actions. To understand the doable nature of an action is to recognize what it needs. When Adler asked us To Hold something, we had to discover what was necessary in order to do that. Since the nature of holding, or of any particular action, is constant, its nature can be understood once and for all. To Hold is To Hold, it is not To Carry or To Throw. However, the actor adjusts the doing of an action according to what Adler called the action's end. The end of an action is that point toward which the action is heading for its fulfillment or accomplishment. In the case of holding, the end is that which the character is trying to hold—a book, a leaf, a baby. The end tells the actor what he needs to do in order to carry out (win) the action. It is the book, the leaf, or the baby, each according to its own life, that tells the actor the adjusted nature of holding it.

Adler said, "The action is in the end." By that she meant that the end is actually what makes the action doable. For example, To Think is impossible until provided with an end: To Think about last night. Likewise, To Count is not doable until provided with an end: To Count the lightbulbs in the room, or To Count the dots on a friend's dress.

The end of an action enables the actor to experience the doing. The dots on a friend's dress enable the actor to experience counting. The end also determines whether the action is relatively easy or more difficult to accomplish (win). The lightbulbs may be easier to count than the dots. But, as Adler explained, the amount of energy required to do an action, whether the action is easy or difficult, is no more nor less than necessary to reach the end. To Count something needs only the amount of looking it takes To Count that thing. If the actor uses more or less energy than is needed, he distorts the nature of the action. Therefore, the necessary amount of energy for an action is also contained in its end. To Climb a mountain takes more effort than To Climb a stairway; To Hold the baby requires more attention than To Hold the book. By focusing on the action's end, the actor keeps the doing of the action sane, logical, and true.

Adler explained that an action also includes "Where I am doing it," since everything occurs somewhere. She described the environment of an action:

> Every action has a world around it. I'm going to count the number of things on the table: a book, a lamp, two pencils, an ashtray, a cup—six. What I am doing most is counting the things on the table. But as I am doing this most, what else is happening around me? I see that there is a white shirt there. That person is moving her hands. There's a gray thing across the chair there. There's somebody with blue on. There's a little bit of red. This is the world around the action. Instead of paying attention to those things, I do my action, letting things happen around it.

Our task was to know and to experience the doable natures of actions so thoroughly that, even as the world around an action would change, we sustained the action's doable nature. Adler said, "The tiniest nucleus of acting that you carry through all your life is that the nature of an action is hard or easy, it has a world around it, and you must try to do it."

Ultimately, to do an action onstage, the actor supplies answers to the following questions:

- Who is doing it? (the character)
- Where is he or she doing it? (the place)

- What is around him or her? (the changing world of the circumstances)
- When is he or she doing it? (the time of the circumstances)
- What is his or her aim in doing it? (the objective)
- For whom is he or she doing it? (generally, the partner)
- Why is he or she doing it? (the justification)

SIMPLE DOING

Adler began the practice of action at the simplest level—doing the small, immediate, physical things of everyday life; for example, To Sew. She pointed out that when a person does a simple physical action in life, he or she can do it automatically because he or she is being fed by the reality of the objects at hand. But, To Sew onstage is not so easy. Prop objects are drained of their reality, and the actor has to invest them with life in order to do actions truthfully.

Since stage objects may be either real things or representations of things (a shot glass of whiskey may actually be a plastic shot of tea), or even imaginary things, Adler taught us to work progressively with objects. We worked first with real objects, memorizing which muscles and to what degree were exercised in using the objects. For example, we repeatedly threaded a needle, getting our muscles to remember holding and manipulating the needle and thread. Then we did the simple action of threading a needle working with so-called prop objects, calling upon our muscle memory, but not necessarily getting the thread through the needle, though treating the props *as if* we were actually threading a needle. Last, we did the threading action working with an imaginary needle and thread. The progression tested our muscle memory, to see if we could execute, normally and with ease, the steps of a simple physical action both with and without real objects.

Elemental drilling in physical realities was, in Adler's opinion, fundamental to maintaining the craft of acting.

> If an actor were really serious, and lived in a serious theatrical community, he would stop acting every five years to repeat his early muscle training—to clean up, to stop the indicating, to see where it has gotten faulty. Musicians do that. They take off six months and go to Switzerland to practice. I lived next to [the virtuoso violinist Nathan] Milstein, and let me tell you, he practiced every day. He practiced scales. He didn't practice a piece. Well, these muscle exercises are the scales.

Adler's technique for working with objects also included sustaining a sense of truth. The muscle movement of a simple action, having been accurately memorized, should not then be mechanically reproduced. As Adler reiterated, just as the actor can take no object for granted onstage, he cannot presume any action to be complete without actually doing every step of it. The actor does not skim over any step if he is to experience, and have faith in, the reality of what he is doing. To demonstrate the actor's sense of truth, Adler picked up an imaginary bottle.

> Please understand that you will never get ammonia on the stage, not in a thousand years. But if you open the bottle, really open the bottle, strangely enough you will be able to have ammonia. But if you don't really open the bottle, then the next

tiny moment of "Phuh, ammonia, oh God, that's strong," will not come. The principle is: When the body is true, the soul reacts. When the body lies, the soul gets frightened.

The audience accepts the actor who is physically accurate. Adler said, "In order to make them believe you, you must do it the way they do it at home." But if the actor indulges in the smallest physical lie, the audience withholds their trust.

It's like on television. When the girl picks up some jar and says, "Do you see this? It's cream," she is always acting a little bit. She is not really doing that tiny, physical thing, so it is terribly hard for her to convince me. In advertising, she doesn't need to. But on the stage, she will never be able to act like that. It is the tiny, physical thing that will release her to real acting.

The idea was to commit, step by step, to the simple physical truth of one action after another, no matter what the dramatic situation. If we could sew onstage—not show sewing—or if we could shave onstage—not do more or less than shaving—then we could take the action of sewing and the action of shaving into any dramatic situation. We could shave in a trench, using a rusty razor and the rainwater at our feet, while bombs exploded in the distance, as long as we had learned what shaving needs. The plots of plays change, but the nature of an action does not.

If you can read the letter, close the window, and put

on your hat and coat, you can play any play I give you around that. You can play that you're leaving home forever, or you're going to the theatre, or you're going out to kill a man. You can play any play if you really close the window, if you really read the letter. But if you are untruthful with the letter, and then say, "Now I am going to kill a man," you cannot go anywhere. You cannot get anywhere. You are physically false. You have to be physically true.

To play the simple truth of the play, from action to action, was, in Adler's memory, the single most important teaching given to her by Stanislavsky. In other words, the foundation of real acting is successively experiencing each half-minute of a whole play. So, in Adler's view, every actor in the modern theatre must become an expert in doing the simple reality of actions, with and without props. The milieu of the modern actor, as she noted, is rarely classical verse theatre, where the language is the priority, but is a theatre of doing.

Your style is what we call the realistic style. In that style, you are generally in a room, some kind of defined place. You are not in Heaven or Hell. You are not in Purgatory. You are not in a Greek temple. You are on a set on this stage. Being on this stage, you must find a way of being able to live on this stage. You must be able to live in whatever physical way I ask you, without talking. You must be able to tie your tie, smoke a cigarette, make a fire, set the table, put your books away, put on a record, fix a drink—all this being very physically easy for you

to do. You must not go to the words first. Always
go to the physical life on the stage, and first see if
you can live on it, with it, without words. Never go
onstage unless you can say, "I am physically true in
what I have to do. I can do one physical thing after
another without words."

Having acknowledged that not all of modern drama is in
the style of realism, Adler contended that, even in theatre
as stylized as that of Jerzy Grotowski, its basis is the actor's
creating a reality onstage. Techniques to keep the stage
reality alive constituted the next level of our training.

Complication of the Doing

The stage, compared to life, is an empty place, a dead
place; it is hard to be there and hard to do something there.
Yet, as Adler said, "Acting is something happening." Something is always happening off the stage; life is complicated,
and never goes quite straight.

Whenever I put on my jacket to go out, my maid is
always brushing things off of it. It means my jacket
has a life. Whenever I pick up the dog's chain, it
is knotted. Something else has hair on it. In life,
objects complicate themselves.

For things to happen onstage, the actor first knows what
to do—the action—and then adds a complication.

In life, if I take a scotch and soda, it arranges itself.
The soda is flat, so I take a fresh bottle. Or I say,
"I just want that much. No thanks, I don't take

ice." Other people do take ice. I know a Hungarian doctor who doesn't trust anybody with his drinks. When he takes a glass, he looks at it, then sterilizes it with his own handkerchief. But on the stage, where everybody is always drinking scotch and soda, there is no life. Even if each actor would only ask himself, "How do I take my scotch and soda?" that would help. But they only do the convention of truth. They drink the stage scotch and soda.

A complication is an obstacle put into the action that impedes it from moving directly toward its end. Adler taught not to pre-decide how to overcome the obstacle, but simply to arrange for the circumstances to present some difficulty in doing the action. To complicate an action is to invest it with reality.

> From now on, never take the simplest road. I want you to decide: "I want to smoke a cigarette, but it's all crumpled, so I have to smooth it out first." Or make the matches wet, so you have difficulty striking them. From now on, do not go to the simplest smoking of a cigarette, but have the control to complicate the simple, baby physical actions.

Many actions, by nature, are already complicated. But every uncomplicated action—every simple physical action—needs the insertion of an obstacle. The complication gets the actor more involved in trying to reach the end of the action.

We practiced with real and imaginary objects, learning to humanize the doing of simple physical actions. For example, before tying a necktie we had to scratch a spot of food off it. To read a letter, we had to extract it from a sealed envelope. To put on glasses, we had to first remove some sticky substance from the lenses. To put on gloves, we had to first brush snow off them. To put on socks, we had to include pulling one out of a shoe and the other from under the bed. When the actor arranges for the props or the circumstances to present obstacles, he allows for spontaneity to arise.

Having asserted, "Your talent is in your choice," Adler encouraged us to choose complications that would cause us to respond emotionally, increasing our need for the action. Also, she wanted the complications to make us move toward, not away from, the end of an action. In other words, an obstacle should not be so great as to make the action impossible or to cause the actor to abandon the action out of frustration. Finally, Adler said to avoid theatricality in our choices. For example, we could have our coffee-drinking impeded by cigarette ashes in our cup, which is possible in everyday life, but not by bugs, which is fantastic. Adler wanted us to choose complications logical to the nature of the objects and probable to the nature of the circumstances, and not go for tricky or clever inventions.

Complicating an action is a major means of living truthfully onstage. Besides making the action more life-like, the complication evokes an ambience, giving the actor a sense of being an artist. Accordingly, Adler referred us to the philosophy of a playwright.

> Giraudoux says that to be able to live in the world, to know little things truthfully and to do them, is one of the greatest accomplishments in life. He says that you must respect God, but live your life. In

other words, the big time is not your picture in the papers. The real big time is: "I'm going to clean my skirt, I'm going to put on my glasses, I'm going to put on my watch—and complicate it! I'm going to put on my watch, and, oh dear, the glass is loose, let me fix it—there." That's poetry. I'm really trying to do my simple, physical action, and the poetry comes out. You don't have to make anything happen. It is there for you. The complication gives you the life. If you live truthfully with this watch, trying to fix it in order to wear it, you'll never be dead, but always alive. There is nothing better.

Complications relieve the props of the look of props, and the action of a mechanized numbness. Complications release the actor to natural impulse, the truth of life.

CIRCUMSTANCES AROUND THE DOING

An action has surroundings, known as the circumstances, of which there are two sets. The larger set answers the question "Where is the play?"—meaning the society and the period in which the play is located. The immediate circumstances answer the question "Where am I?"—meaning the place in which the current action is being done and its effects, including the stage partner. Both sets have been sketched into the play by the playwright. The actor finds the circumstances by reading out from the script—seeing what is there. The actor does not read into the script—imposing what is not there. The actor does not add fiction to fiction. The actor gradually gives body to the playwright's sketch, turning fiction into the truth of life.

THE LARGER CIRCUMSTANCES: Each play has a present time, which stems from a past. The playwright depicts the present and suggests the past. The actor's responsibility is to create a past that is logical to the information given in the play. Specifically, the actor imaginatively constructs a past for the character, mainly so the actor can live knowledgeably in the present, doing and speaking from a viable history.

Adler's technique for creating a past was to Activate the Facts. To demonstrate, she assigned us a sample plot:

> I met Henry in Hartford at the Athletic Club. He phoned me at the General Electric factory in Brooklyn, where I work because I need money, to invite me to his wedding. The wedding of Henry, who attends Princeton University, will be a large, formal, Christian ceremony.

First of all, we had to figure out the nature of our relationship with Henry, including an attitude toward him. The attitude could be "I like him in spite of his faults" or "I have much in common with him." We then had to activate one of these attitudinal facts. To activate a fact is to bring it to life in living color. We imagined ourselves doing things with Henry in various past circumstances, since the past was when we had formed our attitude toward him. Having given a specific background to our relationship with him, we were able to speak truthfully about Henry. For example, if we built a past in which Henry had come over to shake hands after losing our game of racquetball, then we possessed the authentic background experience to say "I like Henry."

Next, we had to construct a background for our character. Fundamentally, Adler taught that no character's background is ever the same as the actor's. The background must be built. Our first step was to ask "To what societal class do I (the character) belong?" We researched the values and general lifestyle of that class, to establish a sense of behavior. Then we imagined ourselves active in the character's everyday circumstances, including working at the General Electric factory: we imagined the layout of the factory and the kind of work we did there day to day, from start to finish. We also imagined living at home, including the look of the house in Brooklyn, both inside and out, and what went on there. And we imagined the space between home and work, the type of transport and the route we took to get back and forth. We tested the viability of our imagined background, first by drawing pictures of it and then by constructing, to some extent, the basic features of the General Electric factory onstage. We found ways to work comfortably, performing simple actions without words. The idea was to live the character's background. In this way, activating the facts of the character's background, the actor experiences something of what made the character who he or she is.

We also had to build a background for Henry. We researched the ethical and political views held by Princeton society and the rituals of a Christian wedding. We needed to understand Henry's way of thinking, based on his upbringing, to see how Henry's thinking differed from our character's. Then, as a living someone replete with a background, with knowledge of the partner and an attitude toward him, we were prepared to respond to Henry's invitation. Creating the past lets the actor respond authentically to the present.

Adler noted that to bring to life the larger circumstances of an entire play is painstaking, perhaps even painful, work. It is, after all, a process of giving birth. Nevertheless, the actor accurately interprets the present only through having experienced the past. Through experiencing the background of the character and knowing the background of the partner, the actor discovers what his character thinks about the partner and consequently what to do about the partner.

Adler said there is no shortcut to creating or "mothering" the larger circumstances. The only way is slow, diligent, careful labor: reading the play, getting impressions and gathering facts, filtering these impressions and facts through the imagination and enlarging upon them in great detail to develop the background. When the actor is alive to the social situation behind the play, he or she can be at home and at ease in the play. It makes no sense to try to respond to the partner through the inert facts (lines) of a script; rather, it is natural to respond through a known history.

THE IMMEDIATE CIRCUMSTANCES: Having remarked that "in life, everybody is a great actor because they accept the ease of circumstances," Adler explained that on the stage the circumstances are neither so available nor so helpful as in life. To be comfortable onstage, the actor creates a fleshed-out version of the circumstances that are merely indicated in the script. Then he grows very familiar with the circumstances he has created.

The immediate circumstances, including the place, the situation, and the partner, exist to impel the actor to do

something. The actor does something about what is happening where his character is (the situation), and the actor
does something about whom his character is with (the partner)—all according to who his character is. As Adler said,
"The action is found within the place." When Adler placed
us in a train station, we found the action To Wait. Where
the character is, and who is with the character in that place,
determines the action the actor/character takes.

Adler referred to the immediate circumstances as "the
now," which, she said, the actor must want. If the actor
wants an alternative time and place, he is not in the play. If
the actor prefers a train station from his own life or the train
station of yesterday's rehearsal or the train station of last
night's performance, instead of the train station logical to
now, the acting is an anachronism. Adler was totally against
putting one's own life onstage or attempting to repeat a
performance. In her view, all the actor could, should, and
must do was an action in specifically created circumstances
experienced for the first time. The now of the play is the
actor's focus and contains all that exists.

Yet it is by the grace and power of the actor's intelligence
and imagination that the now exists on the stage at all.
From clues given in the script, the actor generates the now.
The actor brings to life the props and set pieces, creating
attitudes toward them, investing them with personalities of
their own. The actor creates a world within the immediate
circumstances—a world that has a climate, sounds, smells,
and vibrations, an array of qualities logical to the place.

The immediate circumstances give the actor his action,
affect the manner of carrying it out, and determine whether
he wins it or loses it. To win the action means to carry it out
to its end. Losing it means terminating or abandoning the

action before reaching its end; that is, some factor, such as a telephone call, may enter the circumstances to terminate the action, or the partner may successfully resist the action. When the character either wins or loses an action, there is a transition, and the actor proceeds to the next action. During a transition, the actor thinks or verbalizes the transition or does some simple physical action logical to the place. Whatever the actor does in the transition carries him over to the subsequent action necessary for the subsequent now. As Adler explained, the action changes when and because everything else has changed. She gave the example

> A man is at a party. The lights go out and he seeks to embrace a woman in the dark. The lights come on, revealing that the person in his arms is another man.

The man has lost his action because the circumstances have altered. There is a transition. His next action arises from the new now. The play is played by adjusting to the ebb and flow of one now to another now.

Adler defined acting not as talking but as doing something in a place and letting things happen. To the degree that the actor personalizes the immediate circumstances, making himself familiar with everything there, he has the capacity to let things happen in the place. Being at home in the place, the actor is available to life arising within the place—to complications in the action, intrusions on the circumstances, surprises, things happening for the first time. Accordingly, Adler advised, "Do not become hypnotized by this clinical thing [the doable nature] that I tell you to do in the action." Not to become hypnotized was to select from the immediate circumstances whatever we personally needed to accomplish our action.

> There is a story about an actress in Romania. The Queen had come to see the performance, and just as the curtain was about to go up, the actress, who had been doing some little last-minute arrangement, realized she had forgotten her handbag. She told the stage manager, "I need my bag." He went off and brought back a bag for her. She said, "No, that's not my bag." He said, "Use it anyway." She said, "No, I can't use that bag." He went and got another bag, again not hers, and the same situation was repeated. Then he said, "The Queen is waiting for the curtain." She said, "I don't act for the Queen, I act for me."

The actor selects his or her materials according to the logic of the situation as revealed in the script. The actor's selections nourish his behavior within the given circumstances. For example, Adler asked us to consider what we would choose for Kitty Duval, the innocent prostitute in Saroyan's *The Time of Your Life*, when she is seated in the honky-tonk saloon, dreaming of home.

> What can you use to help yourself? The average choice is a skirt and sweater. But for me, she is a girl who is dreaming of home, and the text says that she has no home. So how does a girl dress who has no home and comes to a bar? How is her hair done? The text says that she used to have a wholesome farmhouse home. Is it good for her now to wear

wholesome clothes if she is dreaming of a time
when her life was wholesome? Would she wear a
skirt and sweater? Put yourself in a similar situation:
"I have nothing around me that has any value, but
I used to be very rich." What serves your purpose in
those circumstances?—sparseness, shabbiness, cold-
ness. If you have nothing now, but used to be a very
beautiful girl, an actress wearing wonderful clothes,
what serves now? A shabby fur coat, leftover finery,
handed-down clothes from showgirls. What is the
color of your hair?—dark at the roots. What is the
quality of your hair?—poor.

Adler taught us to establish circumstances: to walk
around in the place, seeing things through our imagination,
personalizing things, becoming familiar with the place and
relaxed. Familiarity with the circumstances leads to inspired
acting. She said, "Never do anything without the ability to
cross and use the room." Accordingly, she gave us the situation that the character is waking up in his bedroom, and his
simple physical action is To Get Dressed. Instead of having
all the character's stuff at hand, we arranged his materials
so as to have to use the place. We decided that there were
no clean shirts in the drawer, yesterday's shirt was stuffed
in a laundry bag hanging over on the door handle, and the
character's favorite socks were under the covers. We filtered
the immediate circumstances through our imagination, so
as to use the place in a personal way. Personalizing the circumstances helps the actor

- Want to reach the end of his action.
- Reveal something about the character.

- Live in a place where things happen.
- Take the "curse" (weight of importance) off the words.
- Release to a deeper level of talent.

In teaching the use of circumstances, Adler recalled an early experience in acting school:

> They gave us a plot: You're on a boat. The boat is sinking. Your two children have drowned and you can't find your husband. They said, "Do that action." Everybody, including me, went around screaming, "Aaahhhhhhhhhh!"

She promised not to thrust us into similarly horrific situations, but asked us to forevermore be physically able—not emotionally and not verbally—to "answer" [respond to], according to the logic of the place, any given circumstances.

> Stanislavsky said, "If you don't physicalize when you have to do your action, if you don't physically use the circumstances to feed you, the theatre will go down." He would give me three physical things to do in a place. When I did them, I immediately realized how smart he was. I realized that the play [the situation in a place] has to be physicalized enough by the actor to let something come through him. But if you have no play [no imagined circumstances], even if you are relaxed, nothing comes through you. You must never be onstage without a situation, an imaginative situation. You must not be onstage in your situation [from your own life]. It must be imaginative! Otherwise, it is not theatre.

Above all, before talking, before acting, the actor accustoms himself to the situation of the play. Adler's technique for becoming accustomed could read as follows:

- Establish the set, the props, the circumstances. Select everything for the purpose of feeding your ability to do something in the place. Personalize your selections.
- Walk around in the set. Be there to see if movement can be comfortable and life can come in.
- Give reason to your movement. Let surprises, accidents, or choices come spontaneously. The circumstances are there for things to happen within them, and to give the acting its humanity and truthfulness.
- Find the action, including its steps and its end. Know that within its steps there is thinking and doing. Everything—props, costume, set, partner—affects the doing of the action. You win or lose your action according to how the action develops (including its rhythm) in the situation.

When the actor truly resides in the immediate circumstances, he has the right to feel something about the place, the partner, and the situation. That is, the actor has the right to attitudes.

ATTITUDE WHILE DOING

The qualities with which the actor endows the circumstances spark his responses to them. Broadly speaking, the actor's character likes or dislikes the place and the partner.

Adler taught that the actor has to have an opinion of where the character has been before the actor can respond to where he is. For example, if the situation is that the

character is arriving home after a day at the office, his
attitude is influenced by what happened on the way home.
Depending on the play and the character, the actor may
imagine that the way home involved either standing on a
crowded subway being crushed by strangers and getting
a headache, or lounging on a train playing poker with his
cronies and relaxing. Thus the actor comes to the place
already warmed up. Rather than entering the stage set
naked from the wings, the actor arrives fully clothed in an
attitude based on the situation from which his character
came.

Adler asked us to note that every human being has
opinions built in by experience and acculturation, and
that human beings constantly exhibit these opinions on
the street, at home, in shops, in restaurants, etc. A man
will pass a child playing hopscotch in the park; smiling, he
pats her head. A dog barks at a letter carrier; he shies away.
A man propositions a woman on the subway; she laughs
at him. These spontaneous responses derive from each
person's opinion of what the other—the child, the dog,
or the man—is saying and/or doing. Adler commented,
"The wisdom of acting lies in knowing that it is not what
a person says or does but what *reaction* you have to what
he says or does, that creates your attitude toward that person." So, the process is that an attitude gets born, arises
quickly in response to the situation, and is acted upon
immediately. Adler said,

> Ask yourself "Do I have an attitude toward a
> snake?" Where does the attitude come from?—from
> the snake. The snake gives you what to think and do
> about him. Would you go over to a snake and pick

him up? So, from the snake you think something,
and then you know what to do.

An attitude travels. It is carried over from situation to
situation. For example, Adler suggested that if we had
heard that one of the bag-carry-out boys at the supermarket disappointed a girl by keeping her waiting, we
may judge the boy's behavior as unreliable, immediately
creating an attitude of "I don't trust him." Then, if we
were in the situation of giving our groceries to the boy at
the supermarket, how we would tell the boy to find our
car would be colored by our attitude. In other words,
an attitude once formed tends to stick. Adler asked if we
were aware that she had an attitude toward each of us,
that she might take one of us seriously and be amused
by another. Also, she pointed out that each of us held an
attitude toward her, which would guide our behavior in
relation to her even at a party outside the studio, as would
her attitude toward each of us.

She said that, like a person in life, the actor/charac-
ter on the stage is full of attitudes. The actor consults
the script to find the attitudes. The attitudes are only
indicated, ususally not spelled out, in the script. They
are indicated in the character's reaction (the action he
takes) to the place and to what the partner is doing in
the place. For example, the character's reaction may be
To Support or To Destroy or To Ignore what the partner
is doing—each different reaction indicating a different
attitude. Adler insisted that all the character's attitudes
must somehow be physicalized. In the act of supporting
or destroying or ignoring what the partner is doing, the
actor physicalizes his attitude toward the partner. The

audience must be able to *see* what the character thinks and feels about where he is and with whom he is.

Attitudes also set the level or mood of the action, whether it is light (comedic) or dark (serious). For example, if the actor/character thinks the partner is behaving idiotically, he may respond by picking a fight (dark) or teasing him (light), based on his attitude toward the partner. Attitudes bring up ripples of feeling between the actor and the partner. These ripples humanize the stage and instigate drama. Attitudes are responsible for the birth of conflict onstage.

When the actor is stable in the circumstances, he knows the action he needs to take in the place and how the action will be colored by his attitudes. Then he only needs a reason to do the action.

JUSTIFICATION OF THE DOING

The need to do an action is contained in the action's end, but the need begins in the actor. The actor creates a specific reason for doing something in a specific place. This reason revs the actor up to try to do it. According to Adler, justification is the "heart of acting." It pumps the action into circulation, getting it going. Having said that real acting is not playing the play but needing the play, Adler offered justification as the means to really act.

Justification, Adler said, is imaginative rather than logical. It stimulates the actor's creativity. It arises from the actor's insight into the nature of the circumstances. For example, a logical explanation for someone's praying for rain might be that the earth is dry. Although valid, this reason may lack sufficient spark to ignite the action To Pray. A more stimulating reason might be because the children are dying of thirst. The actor selects the justification according to its power to move him. That way, he can really want the action's end (the rain) and can experience the doing (the praying).

Adler asked us to delineate three separate areas on the stage and do a simple physical action with an object in each area. We connected the three areas by providing justification for moving the object from one area to another. We thus realized Adler's teaching that "the situation in the theatre is the place justified."

Justification takes into account the nature of where the actor/character is. Something is happening in a specific place that demands a specific action: we justified the action To Pray for rain by deciding "The children are dying in this dry place, which must be made wet by praying for rain." By choosing the justification according to the nature of the place, the actor performs the action in a rhythm appropriate to the stage, which is different from the rhythm of daily life: although the nature of praying does not change on or off the stage, the actor's justification for the character's praying relates to the potential for drama within the place. The actor's sense of theatricality can be seen in his choice of justification. As Adler said, "Your talent is in your choice."

Justification is what actually allows the actor to Activate the Facts of the play. Justification lets the actor speak the lines not as a journalist reporting, but as a character who (by virtue of the actor's imagination) has experienced the facts. For example, if the text reads "I walked out of the cafeteria," the actor may justify or activate the fact by imagining that the character's ex-lover has walked into the cafeteria. Here again, the justification is not simply logical but is creative. If the actor has to say, "The man got on the bus," he may imagine that it was to flirt with someone (creative justification/activation) rather than to go home (logical justification/activation). Through his choice of justification, the actor gets involved in experiencing some sort of life behind the words of the script. Otherwise, the actor is involved merely in words.

Our homework was to spontaneously and creatively justify whatever we saw happening around us in daily life: Why is someone walking down the street slowly?—because she is searching for money on the sidewalk. Why is someone else walking quickly?—because he is picking pockets. Adler told us to avoid justifications that convey someone's physical condition or emotional state. Thus, the person is walking slowly not because she is tired or walking quickly not because he is hungry. This kind of justification, she said, piles fiction upon fiction and is passive in nature. Instead of involving the actor in the life behind the words, it leaves the actor dry, sucking on the fact.

Using justification to activate the facts of the play, the actor intelligently, dramatically, and sensitively converts the plot from text to experience. The actor is rewarded, according to Adler, with a sense of being an actor—because of having dived into his imagination. The actor experiences himself as a person creating situations, not someone reciting lines.

Ultimately, the actor dramatizes the situation onstage by activating the facts moment to moment and justifying the action within the place. The actor decides, for example, that he is drinking tea not because it is there or it tastes good but because the doctor has ordered it. The actor upsets the humdrum repetition of daily life. The actor turns humdrum daily life into theatricalized daily life, which he experiences.

The Principle is
DO A MILLION LITTLE TRUTHS,
ONE AFTER THE OTHER.

THE THEME IN ACTION

If you do not raise the ordinary fact of the action to a high, universal level, you will be looking for the lines and not for what the author wants to say.

Adler taught us to connect everything done onstage with the theme of the play.

> I want you to draw something epic from the stupid little action of *amo, amas, amat*. Get some idea out of your action that makes it big. You must be objective enough to know that the writer put something in that is very large and very human. Therefore, you must not think of your action as something small.
>
> If the action is To Read a Book while Drinking Tea, you may get the impression of coziness. Then you can lift it by supposing that coziness is something mankind has always wanted. He has wanted to be enclosed in a house and to feel the warmth of being protected. He has found ways of getting that.

Adler offered examples of elevating a simple action to the level of a theme: "Modern opinions and all of modern life is canned" elevates opening a can of tomato soup. "People are tied to traditional behavior" elevates going for a walk. "Hurried work exhausts life uselessly" elevates rushing to meet a deadline. "The world of imagination exists eternally" elevates rehearsing a scene. Having argued that what contemporary playwrights want to say is not written in the lines, as is the case in classical drama, Adler told us to look for the playwright's theme within the situation. In other words, in modern drama it is not the poetry of language but the poetry of doing an action in specific circumstances that speaks the human truth.

According to Adler, modern dramatic themes are concerned with the clash between two elemental human tendencies: the "gimme instinct" and the "search for something higher." Modern plays, she said, dramatize the opposition of these two ways of life, made apparent by a character's internal conflict. For example: Should the character spurn money or acquire it? Should the character reject power as corrupting or seek it?

Adler explained that the internal conflict of the character has to be externalized. The actor somehow connects all his actions (even simple physical actions) to the playwright's theme. In trying to resolve the character's conflict, the actor directly engages in modern humanity's struggle to find out how to live. Adler said, "You must fit the play, not make the play fit you." By experiencing, through externalizing, the character's conflict, the actor fits the play. He becomes an honest celebrant of the play, and not a hypocrite.

> For these kinds of modern themes and actions, you need to pay the price. This is the difference between English and American actors. The English do not pay it. You can see that in their playwrights and tradition. We are closer to the Russians, in that we are interested in what is going on in you, not in what you are saying. Here in America, we experience the action.

Adler taught us to respond not to cues but to the values of the partner, as the partner exhibits them through his or her actions. Watching, listening, thinking, and weighing opposing ideas, the actor does not "sit on" the partner, waiting for his turn to speak. Rather, the actor lives in the circumstances. He answers the partner out of a real need to resolve the conflict within himself and within the situation. His answer—some action illuminating the theme—elevates the pertinence of the play, since the actor is really experiencing the play's problem and trying to solve it.

Having contended that "the audience goes to the theatre for the story and becomes involved because of the conflict," Adler inspired us to explore the ideological depths of the play.

> Unless the actor perceives the conflict of ideas, the play is too small to get him going and the audience involved. The conflict, coming out of the theme and the aim within him [the actor/character], makes the audience understand more about mankind and opposing ways of life. Therefore, in the play, the character must have an aim [relating to the theme] that gives value to all his actions, justifications, and attitudes. Everything he does must be affected by the theme, because the theme is the key to the conflict. Otherwise, the acting is not interesting.

Adler challenged us to become the modern actor, embodying humanity's struggle for a way of life.

The Principle is
REVEAL THE TRUTH THAT IS IN YOU.

THE ANATOMY OF ACTION

*The action is something the actor says "I am going to do,"
and it must happen.*

The actor depends on the action, no matter what, in
each sequence of the play. It is the actor's foothold for a
dependable performance. Without knowledge of what to
do in the circumstances, the actor has nothing but instinct
with which to act, and the acting may collapse. But when
the actor knows what to do, he can guarantee himself a
secure performance, more or less exciting according to the
theatricality of his choices and understanding of the theme.

To know what to do onstage, the actor has to understand
the nature of every action in the play. The nature of any
action, other than a simple physical one, can be understood
in terms of what Adler called its "anatomy." The anatomy
of an action is a description of what the action does. It is
the key to doing the action.

Some actions are close to the actor's temperament or
are part of his daily life, all of which the actor can easily
physicalize without analyzing their natures. But other
actions, like the grand actions found in epic drama (To
Make a Revolution or To Rouse the Troops) or in modern
drama (To Accuse the Neighbor or To Defend the Truth),
as well as less grand though unfamiliar actions, have to be
approached by means of a technique.

First, look in a thesaurus for a synonym that relates
to your understanding [of the doable nature of the
action]. Look to life to find the heart of the action
at work in the world. Look to yourself to find
what you have done when doing that action. Look

> into your imagination. Or go directly to the play
> to understand the nature of the action. You must
> shop—in your own history, your imagination, the
> world, and the play—until you find [the nature of]
> the action.

The anatomy technique isolates the action's deepest doable nature. As a source for the anatomy of an action, the actor's own life is valid, as Adler said, but with a caveat: the actor must understand that his own situation is never the same as the situation in the play. Although an action's doable nature remains constant, its execution is adjusted according to each set of given circumstances. So, the actor may search in his personal past for the deepest doable nature of the action; for example, for the action To Take Care, the actor may remember what he did when taking care of a baby. The actor can extract from that experience the key of the action, which may be To Pay Attention to Its Needs. How the actor felt when he was doing the action in his own life is irrelevant to playing the action in the circumstances of a play. Adler said, "To hell with the emotion. Rather, technically steal the essential doing of the action."

She asked us to put the doable essence of an action into various circumstances, utterly removed from the circumstances in which we had found the action. With the action To Take Care, for example, we took care of a patient in a hospital, flowers in a garden, and vegetables at a grocery— by paying attention to their needs.

Adler said that it is the action plus the going over it that helps the actor accept the play. Still, an action is never repeated exactly, not even in the same circumstances from one performance to the next. Since the execution of an action is not copied from its source (i.e., neither from the actor's life nor from the world), the execution of an action is influenced by the now of each time. Adler suggested that the American Method actor has tended to cheat the playwright and the audience by reproducing onstage his own past actions, situations, and feelings. Opposed to this kind of self-referential acting, she said, "Using the circumstances of the play [to do the action] is what makes great acting. Being in one's own circumstances is what kills acting in America."

Because the actor understands the logic of the given circumstances, he can find the appropriate action and follow a procedure.

> First comes thought. Then physicalization, which is the experience of the thought. It is an experience when your mind and emotion and soul are all working together, when your whole being understands with your whole being what your whole being is doing.

Adler urged each of us to become "a person married to the world for his need to find and know a wealth of actions." She analyzed the doable nature of a whole repertoire of actions, which we learned to experience. She relegated each action to one of three categories: Inner Action, Verbal Action, or Complicated Physical Action (as opposed to Simple Physical Action). In particular, she concentrated on the actions found supporting the themes of modern plays.

INNER ACTION

Adler began with Inner Action, or those actions, poetic in quality, that are born and grow within the actor/character. Inner Actions depend on the actor's ability to see specific, dynamic images. They require the actor to summon "a mental motion picture" (a phrase Adler attributed to Stanislavsky). The actor develops a movie in his mind, projects it outside, and views it there in front of himself, so to speak. In other words, the actor externalizes the movie. Adler pointed to Shakespeare and poetic American playwrights, including O'Neill, Saroyan, and Williams, to find examples of Inner Action.

To Dream is to transcend the immediate circumstances in favor of another place. The person dreaming, becoming so wrapped up in her images of that place there, which embraces everything meaningful to her, barely acknowledges what is in this place here. The dreamer is not a practical person. She would not be aware that the partner needs a coffee refill; she would hardly notice the partner's cup. A time of dreaming is not a time for being busy or bouncing around in the circumstances. The dreamer's body is rather immobile, preferably not so erect, since, as Adler said, "It is difficult to dream while standing up." Physically, the dreamer stretches her whole self toward a definite, central thing—the dream. Psychologically, the dreamer loses the conscious self. So, the actor wanting To Dream opens up to the dreamer within, letting that aspect emerge. The situation is that the actor/character is being quiet, and suddenly her usual self is getting lost as the dream is being found. The dreamer is not mourning and not necessarily sad. She is deferring to the dream. The key to the action is "not to make the dream but to reach it," leaving the place and one's everyday self behind. The dream has its own substance, into which the dreamer enters. It is also in the nature of dreaming for the dreamer to leave the dream and return to it. The dreamer, being neither mentally ill nor sleepwalking, may go freely in and out of the dream, though she prefers being in it. If the actor/character breaks away from the dream—and it may be painful for her to do so—she may still relate to the place or the partner, though without becoming involved. She does not stay away from the dream for long. Until the action is completed, until the dream is fully realized or somehow lost, the dreamer does not go beyond the point where the dream can be resumed. Practically speaking, the dreamer may adjust to any changes in the immediate circumstances. Or she may use the circumstances, if at all, to assist her staying in the dream. "Mostly," Adler said, "the dreamer wants the dream." Adler sent us to Kitty Duval in Saroyan's *The Time of Your Life* and Robert Mayo in O'Neill's *Beyond the Horizon* to work on the dreamer in action.

To Reminisce is a poetic action whose key is to bring back to life something that in reality is gone forever. The person reminiscing reanimates, simply by remembering it, some powerful scene asleep in eternity till now. Reminiscence is a miracle! It is an action "given to the poet, the artist, the soul who cannot bear this world." It is for the person who possesses an extrahuman dimension, who has the magic to resurrect what has died. Reminiscence is possible not by means of words, but by means of the power within the person reminiscing. The nature of reminiscence requires the actor to create in front of himself an extraordinarily felt vision from the past, to which he returns in surrender. The action, according to Adler, may elicit in the actor a sense of achieving some psychic stature, and is an opportunity for the audience to share in a sphere higher than the ordinary, material world. "Reminiscence," Adler said, "is the author's way of saying, 'For Christ's sake, let's get some size into life!'" When reminiscing, the actor forfeits his pedestrian body. He is figuratively lifted off the ground as his mind and spirit stretch toward his re-creation of the past. Because a wonder is happening, his body cannot be rooted and his speech cannot be glib. Rather, he gradually, tenderly, realizes a complete world for which the character has a pristine feeling of joy, pain, and love. Unlike the action of storytelling, during which the actor builds toward a climax for the purpose of spellbinding and captivating the partner, the nature of reminiscing is more passive. The actor does not pull the partner along with him. Although, as with dreaming, he may sometimes include the partner, he does not include the partner with the intent to tell him something. Basically, reminiscence is a solitary action, into and out of which the actor may drift, while losing and recovering his awareness of the immediate circumstances. Thus, when reminiscing, the actor/character has nothing to sell. There is no denouement, moral, punch line, or common sense for him to push. His only objective is to make a special something live again. His attitude toward the action "may be one of amazement that he can remember at all what passed away so long ago." To reminisce, a fully creative action, is "the art of bringing the emotion existing in tranquillity alive in all its glory." Adler referred us to O'Neill, Williams, Odets, and Maeterlinck to work on the action To Reminisce.

To Unmask, a courageous inner action, is a fountainhead

from which stream To Expose, To Reveal, and To Confess. It is to communicate something in all its immediate pain, despite knowing it will not be understood. A stripping-down to the core in front of someone else, to unmask is to relinquish pride. Unashamedly naked, the person unmasking is able to say, "This is what is left of me. Yet, still, I want to give it away." Since it is the nature of unmasking to go unrequited, it is an action peculiar to modern times. That is because, in Adler's viewpoint, every modern human being, who does not overtly fight the degradation and humiliation inflicted by modern life, feels deeply insulted. Yet, since whoever does resist is even more demeaned by the battle, the modern human condition is to not win and to not be compensated. The only honest recourse, then, is To Unmask the remnant that is oneself. In the end, however, there is a positive aspect to the action. Although the partner does not understand the character unmasking, the character himself, through doing the action, experiences an understanding of what is true. The price of wisdom or truth, then, is a soul bared in surrender. That price, Adler contended, is the creative person's payment due—lest he or she suffer the lifetime alienation of fitting in nowhere. Adler held that in order to know the nature of unmasking (exposing, revealing, or confessing), the actor must experience the action. This concept is what she called one of the great acting techniques discovered by Stanislavsky: "You have to go through the pain in order to talk about it." Adler upheld these unmasking actions as the imperative sacrifice, which the actor makes for his profession. Experiencing the unmasking actions is the modern actor's chance for fulfillment as an artist and a human being.

To Expose is that action which, behaving like an X ray,

penetrates the skin to lay bare an essence. Its anatomy is to disclose the truth.

To Reveal works best when the actor inserts an obstacle; for example, "I don't want to reveal this." Its doable nature is to wrench from inside a world of nonapparent and unclear things, pulling against resistance. Revelation precludes telling or reporting to the partner. As with the process of psychoanalysis, it is a case of haltingly descending inside, extracting old and forgotten images in order to clarify and understand them.

To Confess is to make the deepest possible plunge into the inner self so as to bring up the absolute truth of human existence; that is, the truth of oneself in a tragic situation. Confession implies failure. It is recognizing a revelation of fate; for example, "I did it. I could not do otherwise. I didn't know how to take care." It is recognizing the human condition, which is to fail. It is to have nothing left but to confess one's utter deficiency. It is to vomit things up and give way to the gods. Adler said that confession requires a partner. Though he understands that there is no help for himself, the character confessing wants and needs to unmask in front of another, as if to say: "I want you to know me. I have betrayed. I have failed. I have caused hurt. Please forgive me." Adler suggested that we justify confession with an image of some heinous wrongdoing longing to be ripped out of ourselves. Basically, the wrongdoing is a transgression against one's own humanity. Adler offered that the action may rightly erupt into anger, insofar as the anger stays toward oneself and not the partner. "There is no chip on the shoulder," she said. "It is not that lousy shit of 'I'm going to tell you how mad I can get at the situation.'" Confession is basic

spiritual nudity: "I'm stuck with myself. I cannot be different than I am. I'm caught. I'm in trouble. I brought a
faulty instrument. I brought something to life that is not a
whole person." In other words, confession is a completely
modern action, in that the situation permits no solution.
The actor, Adler said, acknowledges his condition—"I'm
trapped." The actor neither begins nor ends the action
with words, but with the internal experience of human
failure. Some awful image surges up within, causing him
or her to vomit words that trail off into inarticulateness,
not knowing what else to do. Adler asked that we dig
down into ourselves to find where in some major area of
our lives we had hopelessly failed and wasted ourselves.
She said, "You cannot help being a killer. Who was the
first killer?—Cain. So there's a killer in all of us, and
nobody can help it. We kill our profession. We kill our
love for human beings. We are all killers." Having lifted
confession to the universal, Adler called it "the big time
of modern acting," and considered it the deepest action
an actor can do. She cited the plays of Chekhov, O'Neill,
Williams, Hellman, and any playwright who discloses a
no-exit theme, as sources for the unmasking actions.

VERBAL ACTION

Verbal Action is the pulse of realism, beginning with
the works of Ibsen. Verbal actions come from conflicts in
ideology. The most sophisticated of these actions take into
account both sides of an issue, neither of which is right or
wrong. Verbal action engages the actor in a search for truth.
Each idea, infinitely debatable, is aired from opposing
points of view, and then the actor as character and human
being is left to choose a way of conducting himself. For

whichever path he takes, especially off the beaten one, a price is paid and a loss sustained.

Adler explained that the largest verbal actions are informed with epic stature as well as modernity. That is because the actor/character experiences being pinioned in a social situation that calls for self-sacrifice. With conviction and faith, the actor expresses the very center of the human struggle for a way of life. It is a kind of expression that can be effected only through a love of truth. Adler familiarized us with a spectrum of verbal actions, applicable to activating the conflicts of ideas found in modern European, British and American playwriting from Ibsen to Caryl Churchill and David Rabe.

To Explain, an action recurrent in life and literature, is analyzed in the context of a progression. At its simplest level, where it means to elucidate a situation, the action requires an obstacle. The actor knows something that the partner does not. The actor pursues his explanation despite objections, since it is within the nature of explanation to carry on—to the point where the action may evolve into To Persuade. Whether explaining or persuading, the actor's need to affect the partner is very real and very sincere. But the emotion of explaining or persuading circulates within the actor's ideas. The mind of the person explaining is cool, like a George Bernard Shaw character delivering a verbal aria. As Adler taught, "When there is a lot to say, it is very directly said." *To Advise* differs from To Explain in that it involves risk. The adviser is aware of another person's potential to be hurt, of which that person is unaware. The anatomy of the action is to persist presenting over the objective truth of the potential harm to the partner, in spite of the fact that the odds are against the advice being taken.

Adler said that a person who is able to give advice is someone who has attained insight from experience. The action
requires a spiritual largesse denoting a level of wisdom. *To
Lay Down the Law* is advice-giving raised to the nth degree.
It occurs when the harm has already encroached upon the
partner. The actor, while cutting off communication from
the other side and pulling no punches, reaches for universal
truths in order to dictate an ethic of behavior for another
human being. Adler said laying down the law is telling it
like it is, primarily.

To Chat, like the action To Explain, can evolve into
more intense actions. Its essence is to make light conversation on a subject of mutual interest. Though there may be
variance in viewpoints, the chatters' level of involvement
and degree of caring is like that of fellow passengers on
a bus. But when the action develops into To Talk Things
Over, as might happen between a teacher and a student,
the stakes are raised. *To Discuss*, the action that forms the
foundation of modern realism, rises above chatting or
talking, since it involves conflict over ideas having some
weight. Also, discussion results in learning—learning the
partner's way of thinking as well as one's own. Discussion
is the playwright's vehicle by which the audience enlarges
and clarifies its own thinking, through hearing and seeing
a problem defined from opposing points of view. The
actor's approach to discussion is, first of all, to cool the
temperament so he can listen and think. Discussion is
not a childishly impetuous "shooting off the mouth."
Rather, it is a "grown-up action" involving exchange.
A person with a viewpoint has made an inquiry, he has
researched the information he is giving away. His attitude
is civilized, not opinionated. The actor, therefore, elevates

the psychic level of the action above "I'm right." He allows for the possibility of his own way of thinking to be adjusted, enlightened, or even to merge with the way of thinking of the other side. The nature of discussion is an honest back-and-forth giving, receiving, considering, and responding with real understanding. *To Argue* is to interpose an attitude of separation between oneself and the partner. The actor/character disagrees with the partner on what is right. The nature of arguing is to just barely catch what the partner is saying. Being not really interested in the partner's opinion, the actor seeks to advance his own tenaciously held viewpoint, packing it with heat and the desire to win. Taken to the extreme of separation, To Argue accelerates into the action *To Fight*, which is a physical confrontation lacking control. Its anatomy is to strike out in every direction, in any manner necessary, to beat the opponent/partner. For another aspect of fighting mentioned by Adler, *To Attack,* she advised imagining ourselves as bombs, since the nature of attack is explosion. Or, like an animal attacking with its mouth and claws, the actor/character uses all his energy to devour the partner. On the other hand, *To Attack with Words* is chilling compared to a fight. Its nature is intellectual. It is calculated, emotionally controlled, and concentrated in one direction. The actor puts his entire mind behind verbalized images in order to devastate the partner's viewpoint.

Adler selected the Verbal Action *To Denounce* for stretching our psychic size and dramatic range. A classically royal action, denouncement belongs to a person of stature and noble bearing, someone who represents a house, community, nation, or kingdom. He may be the general with his army, the monsignor with his flock, the revolutionary with his fellows, the queen with her court. In other words, the denouncer has numbers behind him or her to assist in denouncing the other side. Adler explained that within the nature of denouncement there is a sense of power so substantial that the actor/character can consider himself inviolate. There is also a sense of security so stable that the denouncer can dare to say, "Yes, I know what I'm toppling, but what can you do to me?" The denouncer has a sense of knowing that he can kill. The denouncer takes an attitude of superiority (built on the weight of the group he represents) toward what he believes to be an inferior opposition. Because the denouncer represents a community rather than acts as an individual, he is able to sustain the mentality of triumph. Adler said that to reach the psychic level of denouncement, we had to learn to embody the norm of power. We had to develop a sense of total integration, living in the gut. To do the action's essence, which is to publicly belittle and devastate the other side, demands might and majesty, refined gesture and movement, and the spiritual ability to be as unafraid as a steel ball crashing against a building. The head of the denouncer cannot be hot. The denouncer does not scream. Denouncement, Adler said, wants clear thinking and cool temperament. Recurrent in the history plays of Shakespeare, to denounce is an epic action.

To Arouse, directed at one's constituents, logically follows upon denouncement of the other side. In the plays of Shakespeare, the action is found in an officer's getting his army to rise up and fight. In modern drama, as in Tennessee Williams, it is found in a spirited person's getting some shattered remnant of humanity to rise up and live. As Adler noted, the whole main action of Clifford Odets's *Waiting for Lefty* is to arouse the oppressed working class to revolt. Adler recommended taking particular notice of the society around the action To Arouse. In Shakespeare, for example, the character doing the arousing stands for a segment of society whose ethics, morality, customs, and behavior he has inherited. Therefore, when the King in *Henry the Fifth* arouses his army with "Once more unto the breach, dear friends," his action is backed by "Cry God for Harry, England and Saint George"—the tradition. On the other hand, in *Waiting for Lefty*, where there is not a communal morality, where there is division in the ethical view, the arouser has only himself and an idea with which to stir up followers. Adler explained that, whereas the modern age allows an instigator to say "Let's change the society," the same outcry in a historic period might have brought on the assassination of the provocateur for disrupting the code. The actor doing the arousing needs to adjust the action in accordance with the play's society, whose conditions he must understand absolutely. To be able to impel the group to rise up, the arouser needs to know their way of thinking. He also needs confidence and security, since it is not in the nature of arousal to feel intimidated by the situation or the society.

Adler analyzed the action To Arouse in relation to the themes of modern drama. She examined respectively the position of the arouser and that of his counterpart, the sleeper. The counterpart's condition, she said, is spiritual death caused by consistently responding only to whatever satiates the appetites—food, drink, sex. With his spirituality in abeyance, the sleeper is reduced to ignorance, indifference, negligence, and inglorious speech. The sleeper's stupor, a manifestation of the antilife position of a disintegrated society, derives from the instinct to be bad—to lie, to cheat, to steal, to kill. It is not, however, a personal badness, Adler noted; rather, it is the result of the social sickness of accepting the impression, as a matter of fact, that life is meaningless or empty. The sleeping character, a representation of modern humanity in spiritual coma, is driven to say: "I don't care. I simply don't care. I don't know why, but I haven't any curiosity." In this way, the sleeper experiences the deepest action found in contemporary drama: To Confess; specifically, to confess that he is no longer able to respond to anything. The alternative position, that of the arouser, is a protective one. The arouser's attitude, based on the instinct to be good and fed by a personal code of ethics and morality, is life-affirming. Reacting to the spiritual lethargy of his or her counterpart (the sleeper) and aware of the disease infecting the society, the arouser's action is totally benevolent and nearly impossible: gently, probingly To Wake Up a dead soul.

Adler's analyses of Inner Action, culminating in confession, and of Verbal Action, culminating in arousal, progressively prepared us to tackle the large spiritual themes of modern drama.

PHYSICAL ACTION

Adler taught us to discover the basic behavior of a complicated physical action by doing it in various situations, justified on either a light or a dark level. For example, we discovered the nature of *To Help* by experiencing the doable essence common to helping a friend prepare a dinner party, helping a patient recover from an operation, and helping a person make the correct decision. Adler recommended that at first we imagine ourselves, rather than the character, in the situation in order to get emotionally closer to the action. We asked ourselves, "What would I do here to help?"—the here, of course, being the circumstances of a character. Through practicing the action as himself in the circumstances of the character, the actor gradually merges with the character in the character's situation, instead of continuing to view the character as someone separate. For example, with the action *To Take Care*, we decided to be a doctor taking care of a cancer patient in the hospital. Our process of developing the action was first to justify it, to get it going, on a dark level, that is, on a life-or-death level. Then, so as not to appear as amateur doctors, we researched the technical behavior of the doctor profession, finding out what we would need in order to perform doctor tasks skillfully and with ease. Finally, we asked ourselves what would we do, if we were a doctor, to take care of a person who is dying of cancer.

Once the actor masters a complicated physical action, he needs to give it an ideological boost, so as not to get mired in the routine procedure of the action. The actor as doctor, for example, could lift the care-taking activities by doing them for the purpose of salvaging and aiding the recovery of human life in crisis. A physical action, supported by a big idea, gives it an elevation worthy of the stage.

Adler concluded our study of complicated physical action with the widest, deepest, and most complex of all physical actions, that is, the action *To Escape*. Having surmised that we might personally be unfamiliar with the nature of To Escape, Adler asked us to spy on the action at work in the world. For example, we could catch its doable essence by observing the exertions of a cockroach trying to escape a kitchen sink flowing with tap water. Basically, we imagined the situation as: The cockroach has no place to go. In every direction, at every turn—flung, drenched, sucked toward the drain, slipping, sliding, crawling, climbing, falling, groping—everywhere, the cockroach fails. Yet, giving its all, the cockroach attempts to escape until it no longer can. Thus we discovered that the anatomy of the action To Escape is to run from one danger into another unanticipated danger into another, constantly threatened by loss of life. It is an action so seldom completed, so consistently unsuccessful, that it nearly always, Adler explained, results in the death, or at best the defeat, of the character. When practicing the action, we were instructed to imagine the circumstances so perilously full of obstacles that they stood almost 100 percent against the possibility of escape. In fact, Adler said, the circumstances around the action are essentially inescapable. For example, if there are waves, they are swelling to fifty-foot heights. If there is fire, it is burning every exit. If there is shooting, it is from every direction. The actor trying to escape fills the place with enough imagined disaster that, without losing control of his senses and the action, he is compelled to run for his very life. Adler noted that the action To Escape can be found in the lives of characters whose situations threaten a doom other than death. She cited the case of Medea, whose initial action is to escape from tormenting thoughts by fighting them off, as well as Hamlet, Ophelia, and Macbeth, each of whom aims, she said, to escape (none of whom does alive) from his or her menacing circumstances. In modern drama, the action To Escape may be found in a character's trying to escape the perils of materialism endangering the life of her spirit, as is the case with Alma in Tennessee Williams's *Summer and Smoke*.

We thus rounded out our experience of Inner Action, Verbal Action, and Physical Action by reaching the pinnacle life-or-death action in each group: To Confess, To Arouse, To Escape.

The Principle is
TO UNDERSTAND AN ACTION, BE ABLE TO DO IT IN A THOUSAND CIRCUMSTANCES.

THE EMOTION IN ACTION

In life, feelings are run-down. We speak without meaning and pretend the words.

At the beginning of our training, we predictably thought that acting is feeling. Adler corrected the misunderstanding. Acting is doing. But when imagination is applied to doing the action, feelings emerge. Adler taught that it is useless to attempt to feel. Making an effort to emote, which she called "pushing" or "squeezing," was the surest indication of bad acting or a lack of technique. To play the mood (and she noted that "mood spelled backwards is doom") or to suffer the emotion is to act without an action, that is, without a foundation.

Adler did not ignore emotion or states of being. Rather, she taught the technique of finding physical means through which to release the expression of emotion or a state of being. For example, if the text reads "It's cold in this room," the actor has to believe in that condition. Adler's solution was to close a window, put on a sweater, or build a fire in the fireplace. The actor does a simple physical action to deal with the cold, and in so doing he believes in the cold. In other words, by buttoning up his overcoat, the actor is able to speak the line not as an empty fact but out of the experience of dealing with the cold.

The same technique is used for a line describing a personal condition; such as "I've got a splitting headache." The actor physically braces himself against the pain. He presses his hands into the table, or his feet into the floor, or his spine against a chair, in response to the pain. His headache line gets delivered out of the experience of dealing with a headache. Adler also taught Stanislavsky's As If technique, which she considered useful for expressing pain. In order to speak about a toothache, the actor imagines feeling, for example, As If a razor were cutting into his jaw. Adler said the actor is not so concerned with actually feeling temperature or pain, but must be very concerned with responding to them.

On the other hand, the actor may have a line describing the condition or emotional state of someone else; for example, "When he saw the phantom of Christmas Past, Scrooge was astonished." In this case, Adler's technique was for the actor to imaginatively observe Scrooge in his circumstances, seeing what Scrooge is doing in response to the phantom that would lead to considering him astonished. Scrooge could be imagined leaping from his bed, crashing into the door and pulling at its bolts and locks; or he could be seen dashing across the room to hide under his bed. The actor imagines Scrooge engaged in activity; such as, in a struggle to escape the phantom. The actor does not imagine Scrooge standing there with an astonished face. The actor speaks the line truthfully out of having actually become involved in Scrooge's dilemma.

The actor needs a specific means of expression for any emotional state. He must not float in a general mood onstage. To this end, Adler taught the anatomy of emotion. Our homework was to hunt for emotions in our lives and in the world. Then we worked backward from the emotion to locate its source in action. So, the actor identifies an emotion and visualizes what the person was doing that caused the emotion to emerge. This way, the actor captures the specific doable nature of an emotion. Doing its nature releases the emotion in the actor. At the same time, the actor takes on the demeanor of emotional truth.

Adler offered To Hold On To something or someone as the doable nature of love. The nature of love stems, she said, from a shared past (or, in the case of acting, an imagined background) of caring for and about the beloved. She noted that loving the past, in the sense of To Hold On To the past, pervades the entire fourth act of Chekhov's *The Cherry Orchard*. Likewise, a feeling of love may be revealed through a character's holding on to his beliefs, that he has cared for, which is, as Adler noted, a dominant action in the life of Shaw's Saint Joan and Ibsen's Dr. Stockmann. Saint Joan and Dr. Stockmann cling to their beliefs despite the threat of death or the impediment of public shame. Their action reveals their love for their beliefs.

Once the doable nature of an emotion has been found in life and understood, it can be transferred to any situation onstage. For example, if the situation is that the character's dog has been hit by a car and he is taking it to the veterinarian, the actor imagines a past of caring for the dog. This shared past enables the actor to cling to the dog's life, holding on to it, trying to keep it—and through this action, the actor reveals (and authentically feels without trying to feel) his character's love for the dog.

Adler gave us a sampling of the doable nature of emotion:

- Sadness—to disconnect from, not taking in, the cause of the sadness.
- Suffering—to attach deeply to someone or something lost.
- Shock—to withdraw or to hide from the cause of the shock.
- Anger—to face, to try to control, or even to annihilate

something, not by means of the anger but by a tremendous power which angered people feel they have.

- Rage—to strike out, wanting to break, wreck, and kill the cause of the rage.
- Boredom—to want to get rid of things and get away from oneself.
- Embarrassment—to recede, holding back from things, people, and situations because nothing, not even to say hello, seems simple.
- Fear—to be unable to face the source of the fear.
- Joy—to explode out toward the source of the joy.

Adler contended that, by virtue of the actor's imagination, theatre is more emotionally truthful than life. Words uttered off the stage, she surmised, are rarely felt or wholly believed. But on the stage (where the actor physicalizes the doable nature of emotion and where the actor physically responds to conditions and states of being), words come alive. Onstage, through imagination and physicalization, the actor can believe in himself and make himself believable.

The Principle is
THERE IS NO GENERAL EMOTION
ONSTAGE.

CHAPTER IV

Characterization:
Who the Actor Becomes

When Stella Adler taught characterization, which extended over the second year of actor training, she invoked the ideas of Michael Chekhov, a noted character actor throughout his life. She concurred with Chekhov's belief that, for the actor to nourish his gifts and sustain an interest in the art of acting, he must characterize. She also agreed with Chekhov that most actors do not. The average actor exhibits his own attributes, values, and offstage situation, playing himself as a type over and over again. It might have been that in the beginning he was praised as an exciting, unusual personality. But once having experienced success he repeated his initial way of acting, as if always painting a self-portrait. He denied himself access to his imagination, talent, and alternative resources. He became tired, and his wages, Adler said, ended up being paid not for acting but for reciting the words of a script.

The actor who confines himself to a narrow career forsakes the joy of acting, which is to change oneself. Adler recalled the story of an actor from her own family who turned her talent into an emblem.

I had a cousin who was a great star in the American theatre. [Katharine] Cornell played with her.
Tallulah [Bankhead] played with her. She was a
little bit ahead of them, maybe five years older.
Her name was Francine Larrimore, and she was
Miss Enchantment. She was born in Russia, but
came here early enough to get rid of the accent
and develop this wonderful kind of American
thing. She was the Most American. If someone
wanted Miss America or Miss Chicago, she was it.
That was her great fortune. She had a red carpet, a
Rolls-Royce with gold fittings, and was absolutely
the star of stars. But she grew older, and when
you grow older you cannot do that Miss America thing. I mean, it's silly. But she couldn't stop
doing it, and because she never could give up that
star personality, life was very hard on her.

Adler explained how difficult it is to relinquish a personality that has been applauded. "That's what people are
coming to see," she said. But knowing that "life says you
must change," she considered monotype acting unnatural.
The actor's path to personal truth and artistic development
involves alteration, effected by exploring a whole variety of
types and creating an individual within the type.

Adler taught that "the live character is the true center
of theatre art," and is brought into existence because the
actor has established the differences between himself and
the character. Fundamentally, the character is a total mask
worn by the actor. Paradoxically, the more entirely the
actor constructs the mask, the more his own inner self
is unveiled. Adler thus postulated that "character acting

permits you to reveal through another person what you have been conditioned to hide in real life." But without the mask, the actor becomes frightened. Instead of revealing himself through an imaginary character, he conceals himself behind stage conventions, not contributing his own human truth to the theatre.

Adler explained to us that even though we may show little of ourselves to the world, we have within us all the characteristics of humanity, like all the statues inherent within a block of marble. She taught, for example, that even if someone is a generally irresponsible person, never on time for an appointment, he can still portray Mr. Reliable. To find the pulse of this character, seemingly unrelated to his everyday self, the actor asks in what situation from his past could he have been judged absolutely reliable. Once he recalls where in his own life he has demonstrated reliability, the actor extracts the essence of what he did then. Amplifying and activating this essence, he transfers it to the circumstances of the play. In this way, the actor is free to say, "I have reliability in me, so if I expand it I can be Mr. Reliable."

Characterization is about the actor's recognizing his universality, rather than displaying his usual aspect, as Adler noted.

> You are everybody. In some area of your life you are a killer, a crook, a liar, and a whore. You are a genius, a god, and pure. You are everything. There goes a man who is going to be killed. There goes you. Somewhere, you are that man.

By learning to perceive characters as not separate from ourselves but as manifestations of our shared human potential, we got over judging, patronizing, belittling, or disliking a character.

To illustrate the scope of characterization, Adler pointed to the versatility of a former student.

> Take an actor like Marlon [Brando]. Do you realize that he cannot be typed? He has a range that, I think, is larger than any actor we have seen on the screen. He is the Godfather, the Waterfront, and the Irish Peasant. He can play anything, everything. How long would his career have been if he had only talked like dis? You know, he does not talk like dat. He was brought up a military-academy boy and his English is absolutely distinguished.
>
> When he played Stanley Kowalski, he changed everything there was to change: his neck, his feet, his teeth, his eyes, his hair, and each thing that he changed affected him. I went to see him in the dress rehearsal [of *A Streetcar Named Desire*], and afterwards I went backstage. But he wouldn't see me, because he didn't yet have that speech, that particular thing that was Stanley Kowalski, that lazy mouth. When I returned for the opening night, there was a complete character. He had taken the part along with the whole play and had put it in his pocket. Now, you must understand that *Streetcar* is not Stanley Kowalski's play. It is a play about Blanche DuBois. But for poor Blanche, there was nothing. There was just Stanley Kowalski.

To Adler there were basically two kinds of performers: those who transform themselves and those who do not.

Her dictum was that "you cannot play yourself onstage, if only because yourself is too unenergized." Though she noted that one job of the director is to help the actor create the live character, knowing the actual conditions of commercial theatre she advised developing the ability to characterize on our own.

> Today, in your theatre, there is no training for characterization, and none of the people outside [of the Conservatory] will help you with it. You simply have to make up your mind to have a range of parts that you can play. I want you to play parts that demand absolute characterization. You cannot play the Devil without being costumed in character. You cannot play Puck, you cannot play Caliban without it. I want you to take parts for which you have to say, "There's nothing about me that I can use. I have to change everything. I have to die." Take big, big parts. Take Peer Gynt. He has nothing that you have. You will have to change.

Characterization means changing oneself to fit the character. It does not mean changing the character to fit oneself.

Character According to Type

Maturity in acting is to understand another person.

When approaching a role, according to Adler, the actor first catches the framework of the type. No matter how unique the character, onstage he must be recognizable as belonging to some type or group of humanity. A type is a category into which characters put themselves, based on choices they have made. Generally, a character's type is determined by his profession or by what he does mostly in life. The character may be an artist type, an impresario, a politician, a preacher, or a mother. The type can also be determined on a behavioral basis, as in the slut type or the dork type.

Adler asked us to search in life and in literature for recurrent types and study them in their environments, noting their characteristics.

> You immediately get something from the word bitch. Anybody can see a bitch. If she's put onstage, she's a bitch. If she's in the movies, she's a bitch. If she's in a room, she's a bitch. You know her, don't you? She's a type.
>
> The bitch will create in you a need to go somewhere in life where you can find her and watch her. The first thing to do is to go down to Tenth Avenue. Go into the cafés and watch. Go over to any cafeteria on Eleventh Avenue. The range of types of that society around the wharves where the boats come in are all there. If there is a tough-guy type, you immediately see that he walks tough, talks tough, and lives in a tough society. Get the voices, the way they sit, what they order, and what they think as a general type.

In other words, a spectrum of types makes up a society. A sub-society (for example, the waterfront society) is a stratification of the larger society (for example, the blue-collar society) from which it takes a social, an economic, a political, and a moral viewpoint. These viewpoints may be reworked by the sub-society according to its own needs. Therefore, the way of thinking on marriage and family, money, government, and conduct of a type (for example, a tough guy) derives from the values of the larger society passed on to his sub-society. His lifelong aim, his direction or purpose, as well as his day-to-day activities, are handed to him by the society to which he belongs. So, a specific character within the type will basically be for or against the viewpoints and values of his society.

Adler illustrated the patterned thinking and uniform behavior of a sub-society she called the Ivy League or WASP society, whose aim, she said, was to maintain the status quo.

I have a home near Southampton [on Long Island], and all the people there are absolutely Anglo-Saxon. There is not an Italian in the lot. I don't know where the minorities hide. I don't know where they put the Jews, where they put anybody.

I went to a party there and I felt, "These are corpses, mental corpses." All of them are wealthy, and as a result, what happens regarding their thinking is that they never exert themselves. Life comes to this particular crowd the same way food comes, the servants come, money comes. There is no effort. It's marvelous. They never talk about anything but "our land, our children, our parents." They have land in perpetuum. Nobody else can buy or sell their land. So they have a great sense of control over something that is unchangeable, and it has affected that group. Being with them was like having doughnuts. Every one is the same.

Adler offered no single, sure avenue of approach to realizing the character as a type. What she did offer was the stipulation that, whichever way an actor takes, his effort needs to result in a character type with an outside and an inside.

Her way of approaching the type from the outside involved shopping in the world or in our imaginations for the appearance of the type. For example, we imagined the grande dame type as tall, large, and ample-chested. She holds her hands at a cinched waist above wide hips. Her chin is lifted and her eyes are made-up. She is decorously costumed, copiously bejeweled, and her hair is intricately done. Keeping this image in mind, we slowly and gradually relinquished our own physical attributes to those of the grande dame. We experienced the ability of our own body to assume the rotundity, height, and weight that permits the grande dame to walk, sit, stand, and move in the manner of taking up space. We then imagined ourselves inside the grande dame's body, doing simple physical actions (such as eating, dressing, writing billets-doux) in the grande dame's circumstances. Doing simple physical actions in the circumstances of the type lets the actor penetrate the personality of the type. The actor may discover that the grande dame's conduct is domineering and demanding, that she is temperamental, that her way of thinking is self-referential. In physicalizing the outside of the type, the actor catches a certain rhythm of behavior, which leads to the attitude, the inside of the type.

Alternatively, demonstrating an internal approach, Adler began with the mentality of the absentminded professor type. We imagined his way of thinking as abstract and disconnected. Living, as he does, mostly inside his concepts, he is unaware of his surroundings. He is eccentric, not in tune with average behavior and out of step with the rhythm of everyday activity. Uncomfortable with things, he is not quite at home anywhere in the physical world. We then took the professor's dissonance and lack of awareness, and let these qualities affect doing simple physical actions in the professor's circumstances. In this way, the professor's appearance and manners emerged. We found, for example, that to study his tomes the absentminded professor uses thick spectacles, which become of no use to him in focusing on the world. He seems to be forever searching for something over or under his glasses. To do his research, he surrounds himself with mountains of notes and books, though he cannot quite put his hand on the item he specifically needs. His papers are everywhere, falling from drawers, bags, and his pockets. In concentrating on concepts, the absentminded professor forgets his body. His necktie is askew, his suit crumpled, his hair a shambles. In physicalizing the inside of the type, the actor catches a mental rhythm, which leads to the behavior, the outside of the type.

Other than going into our imaginations, we could go into life to find the inside or outside of the type. Adler advised us to shop in the world for some object, or to shop in nature for some creature, that struck us as similar to the type. For example, something about the attitude of a bus fit our sense of the boss type. So, from the bus's point of view, everything around is infinitesimal and inconsequential. The bus seems to remain untouched and unaffected by its surroundings. It pushes ahead on its own course, regardless. Or, for the dumb blonde type, we found inspiration in a butterfly, a lightly flitting thing in love with bright objects.

Or, we based the behavior of a zealous enlisted-soldier type on the pesky manner of a bumblebee bothering a blossom. Adler noted that "Zero Mostel made a whole career out of playing a flower." Adler's technique for building the type from real life was, essentially:

- Find something similar to the type in the world or nature.
- Steal some quality of its behavior.
- Physicalize the quality by doing simple physical actions without words in the circumstances of the type.
- Take on only the quality and not the entire image.

In other words, the actor does not become a bus; rather, he assumes the attitude of an image, becoming a bus-like boss. Then, if in characterizing the boss type the action would be To Bawl-Out a clerk, the actor can help himself by doing the action in the manner of a bus confronting a Volkswagen. To build the character as a type, the actor observes and draws on any and all of the behaviors on display in the world.

INDIVIDUALIZING THE CHARACTER

Adler wanted us to stretch as far from ourselves as possible. To get away from ourselves and to get into the individuality of the character, we were to go through the script line by line, contrasting ourselves to the character. Specifically, we were to ascertain

- How the character's *mind* is different from my own. Does the character's mind, for example, work more

quickly or slowly, more precisely or vaguely, more
covertly or openly?

- How the character's *temperament* is different from my
  own. Are the character's feelings, for example, warmer
  or colder, more or less passionate, more or less loving,
  more effervescent or more controlled?
- How the character's *will* is different from my own. Is
  the character's will weaker or stronger, more or less
  tenacious, more or less capable of achieving an aim?

We were to let these differences seep into ourselves.

Adler said that Stanislavsky believed the theatre must get
rid of people who do not perform the play through character. Just as there was never Stanislavsky onstage, there must
not be oneself onstage. Adler assured us that Stanislavsky
worked hard to understand the profound differences
between his own way of behaving and that of the character.

> When you read Stanislavsky's breakdown of Dr.
> Stockmann from [Ibsen's] *An Enemy of the People*,
> you can see where he got the man's exuberance—
> from the childishness in him. I mean, Dr. Stock-
> mann is a child. He is overgiving, overtruthful, and
> a little bit stupid. So Stanislavsky got him from the
> point of view of his emotion [temperament].
>
> On the point of view of Stockmann's mind,
> [Stanislavsky] is brilliant. [According to Stanis-
> lavsky's breakdown,] Stockmann thought other
> people would understand him. He thought if he
> just went out and said, "It's not fair," that other
> people would understand him. He thought if he
> said to a wealthy man, "People are starving and

need food," that that man would understand him. That was stupid.

So, in this way, Stanislavsky built him. He failed, by the way, in this character, and then worked on him for ten years. When he played Stockman again, he understood him. You do fail in character, and then you find it.

We explored the three aspects of character differentiation.

MIND: Since the nature of a person is reflected in his thinking, the actor can approach a role through grasping the mind of the character. Adler illustrated how people's ways of thinking affect their behavior:

> The dean up at Yale never goes all the way out [to another person]. He is very delighted to see you, but then immediately must have an idea to follow. The idea pulls him back into himself. Actually, he is much more at home with being alone than being with you, because with you he has to do something more. So, his way is to say, "Oh, I'm so glad to see you. Ah, yes, you must come to dinner. What day are you here?" His whole way of thinking is having to make the next thing happen.
>
> Now take somebody else, somebody very exuberant. He says, "Hello! How are you?" giving you everything, because as soon as that is said, he's finished with you. He says, "Darling! Oh, you're such a doll," and then asks, "Where's the coffee?" His whole way of thinking is to be done with things.

The actor figures out the character's way of thinking

in order to create attitudes for the character. The actor/character has an attitude toward each partner and each thing within the given circumstances. Adler explained that, whether the actor is Laurence Olivier working almost completely from the outside or Marlon Brando who (Olivier said) begins with the inside, attitudes are what unify the character's outside and inside. The character's attitude toward her situation determines what she will do about it, and what she does about it reveals who she is. Adler proposed the situation that if a house is on fire and everybody runs except for one person who sits down, an attitude has given birth to the nonconformist. Or if two people are waiting for a bus, and one has her change for the fare all set in her hand but the other has no idea how much the ride costs and no money in her hand, then the manager and the flake are born from their attitudes.

Adler illustrated the significance of attitude in individualizing the character.

At the Moscow Art Theatre, I saw a production in which maybe fifty or sixty peasants were onstage with the Prince, who was talking to them, giving the land away and telling them "no more serfs." They were all listening to him, but one of them was looking at the Prince's coat. And out of those fifty or sixty people, this one peasant—he had blue eyes—was standing there not saying anything. But the way he was looking at the Prince!—his eyes were swimming with admiration, as if he were looking at a beautiful woman. It was as if he were saying, "Aiii, if only I could just touch his coat!"

Now, in that audience were Harold Clurman,

Lee Strasberg, and myself. And all three of us went out asking, "Who was that actor?" He was among fifty or sixty people, and he just stood there, dressed like a peasant, with peasant hair, but there was so much love in him—that kind of Russian love you hear about was in his eyes—for that coat, that you could not avoid seeing it. It was as if he were playing Hamlet, he had so much.

Having noted that, in general, the attitude toward things is missing in performance, Adler said that the actor needs to know whether a prop is boring or interesting to the character and whether his bread is tasty or not. The actor's attitude toward each prop—broadly, whether the character likes it or dislikes it—and toward each partner—broadly, whether the character is or is not on the partner's side—has to be made clear. The character's attitudes must be able to be seen, through what the actor is doing, not through what the actor is saying. Everything the actor does contains one more step toward revealing the mind of the character. So, at the end, according to Adler, the audience can say, "I know who he is and how he thinks."

TEMPERAMENT: Adler pointed out that characters, just like real-life people, express their feelings differently. One character may exude emotion. Another may repress her feelings, denying their existence. Yet another may suffer them internally, withholding expression. Adler compared the degree of emotion expressed by her niece, Pearl Pearson, a teacher at the Conservatory, to the emotional expression of another teacher.

The words that Pearl uses do not fit her emotion.

They are inadequate for what she has [feels inside].
Whenever an actor who was a student here comes
back to visit, she says, "Hello. Ah, sit down. Ah, oh,
how are you?" These are not the words she wants to
use. What she wants to say is, "Joy! Joy has come!
Everything is shining and bright!" Pearl is never
just saying hello. It is always more than that, and
the words are not suitable.

On the other hand, there is a marvelous English
woman, a teacher. She says, "How do you do?
Hello, I'm delighted to meet you, Miss Adler. Well,
I'm just thrilled to see you." I don't know what she
means by that. The words are much more than she
has [feels] emotionally, much more. The words are
really very exciting, but she sacrifices her inside to
the words. There is an emotional control.

In general, the actor discovers the character's temperament through discovering how the character feels about
his situation.

WILL: The will of a character relates to his aim in the life
of the drama and how he pursues it—with what clarity of
direction and with what amount of energy. A stubborn person, whose will is strong, will go to any lengths to get what
he wants. An impressionable person, whose will is weak,
may be diverted from his aim. Adler described a vacillating
person, lacking in will, losing his aim:

> You may say, "I want to be an actor. I'm very emo-
> tional. I adore the theatre. But I think a little bit
> slowly, and you talk so fast. I can only take in one
> thing at a time. But I love acting. I love people.

> But, gee, my father wants to give me a car. I have
> to think about this."

As an alternative, she pictured a will staying its course:

> There was a time when I was offered a tremendous
> sum of money. I would have been able to leave you,
> and you could have studied with Lee Strasberg.
> I wanted it very much, but I didn't have the will
> to go. I was afraid. I was afraid that if I did that, I
> would break.

There is always some level of will influencing the behavior of
the character, helping him or her achieve his or her aim or
not.

Adler inspired us to use our imagination to individualize
a character. For example, exploring the aspect of will, we
imagined a weak-willed person with rather trivial goals.
Lacking confidence in his resources, this fellow is forever
scavenging for outside assistance and can be led by the
nose. He is like an insect, a narrow-minded creature always
hankering after something. Getting closer to this character, we imagined the life of an insect, a kind of precarious
existence constantly full of troubles and woe. The insect
always needs to get into something, if only because itself is
so negligible, though nothing ever proves satisfactory since
everything is overwhelming. We then extracted a useful
quality, the insect's attitude toward the environment, from
the image of the insect and put this quality into human
form. We enacted "I'd like to sit down, but the chair is
over there. Maybe I'll just stand here. But oh, the light's
shining on me, so possibly I ought to move in the other

direction. But the floor is slippery. Oh dear, oh well, perhaps I should just try to put on my coat again and go out. But, oh my, there was such a big step when I came in. Oh heavens, I don't know what to do." We discovered that every task this ineffectual character attempts to accomplish seems gargantuan, terribly difficult and fatiguing, until he just lets the activity die away. In building an insect-like will, the actor may arrive at an individual within the browbeaten housewife type, or salaried employee type, or petty aristocrat type.

So, Adler's way of fitting into the character's shoes was to discover the nature of the character's mind, temperament, and will. To make these discoveries, we were to live the character's daily life, doing simple physical actions in the character's imagined circumstances. We were to spend a day with the character, observing the manner in which the character would do things—his way of eating, washing, sleeping, reading the paper, boiling potatoes, blowing his nose, tying his shoes—different from the way we would do things. We were to let these differences affect us, especially our body and our rhythm. Thus, by living daily life in the rhythm of the character, the actor learns a lot about the character's mind, temperament, and will. Through external doing, the actor experiences the character's internal thinking, feeling, and willing.

Adler instructed us, in building a character, to study and to use the same sources that writers, designers, and all artists use: books and magazines, street life and domestic life, the worlds of animals, insects, plants, and objects. We were to stimulate our imaginations by looking for images of the character outside ourselves. She presented questions that an actor needs to pose:

- To what type does the character belong, and what are the viewpoints of that group?
- How does the character think, and what does the character think, particularly about his or her situation and the values of his or her society?
- What is the nature of the character's temperament?
- How strong is the character's will, and what is his or her aim?
- What animal or object is the character like?

Adler encouraged us to change ourselves, to go ahead and make fools of ourselves, to get rid of a sense of shame. She wanted us to give up our customary postures. She wanted us to raise a shoulder, impede our speech, or get a limp. Any way of walking, she said, was preferable to our own. For the actor to physicalize the mind, temperament, and will of a character, he erases his own habits and mannerisms, transforming himself.

Coloring the Individual

Beyond individualizing the mind, temperament, and will of the type, the actor colors the individual. A character's colors are his or her personality traits, stemming from a main character element. The character reveals these colors or traits through his or her choices of, and approaches to, action.

When the actor reads the play, he gathers impressions about a character. He pays attention to what others say about the character and what the character says about himself. He looks for what the character does in response to his situation. Generally, the actor states these impressions as traits or qualities, as adjectives. These adjectives need to be translated into doable activities or actions. If, for example, the character is said to be charming, the actor can choose things for his character to do which enable others to be charmed by him. If the character is said to be efficient and happens to be a nurse, then the actor can arrange and clean the instruments for surgery in an efficient manner. If the character is said to be superficial, the actor can select the action To Chat, but not the action To Discuss, in that discussion has depth. By translating traits into doable activities and actions, the actor brings the character's insides to the outside.

Adler proposed a character trait for us to activate in a variety of circumstances. The idea was to find out what the trait does. For example, with the trait "mean," we could do mean things, like tear up a letter from a friend asking for a favor, thereby discovering that what meanness does is cut itself off from giving to the human need. Adler likewise asked us to activate the opposite of the trait, so as to experience what the trait does not do. Taking the trait "nice," we discovered, through the activity of playing cards, that nice wants to bring enjoyment to the game, while mean wants to beat the others. We learned to physicalize the doable nature of both sides of a human tendency.

Adler also proposed a character type, and asked us to discover his traits or what made him the type he is. For the salesman type, she suggested that, in his mind, everything is saleable. She said that he could be built "bigger than Barrymore, going a mile a minute not only to sell the very air, but also to make the very air in order to sell it." He is upwardly bound, going forward on a progressive path, disregarding tradition. He ignores the small fry. He is practical and does not dream. He is a doer; and if the salesperson is a woman, there is something masculine in her jaw, stride, or the square of her shoulders. In other words, the traits that make the character the type must be visible in his or her body and in what he or she does.

Another exercise was to take a character trait, imagine what type might have this trait as a main element, and then activate the element, seeing where it would lead us. In taking timidity, for example, we determined it to be the main element of the innocent-girl type, activated as To Shrink, To Retire, To Close Up, and To Hide from others and the given situation. We discovered that timidity withdraws into its tiny self, not wanting to participate in the world and not willing to touch life in a big way. Its mind thinks, "I'm threatened." It is fragile, unable to withstand the bold things of life. It pulls its eyes and senses inward, away from stimulation, away from the daring and powerful. Therefore, its way of contact is indirect and conditional, its way of communication is circuitous and hesitant, its way of movement is tenuous, and its way of walking is not rooted to the earth. Discovering all this about timidity was to discover the nature of Laura in Williams's *The Glass Menagerie*. So it goes, that once the actor is able to experience the doable nature of timidity in imagined circumstances, she can activate timidity in Laura's circumstances, performing Laura's play.

Alternatively, we took an already existing character, ascertained his or her main character element, and not only discovered its doable nature but also caught the universality of its doable nature. The point was that once the actor has nailed the behavior of a character element, he can transfer the behavior from the circumstances of one character to the circumstances of another similar character. To demonstrate, Adler turned to Nora from Ibsen's *A Doll's House*, whose central element Adler identified as childish, colored with the traits of naiveté, credulity, and amazement. Not wanting to grow up, Nora plays at being a wife and mother. Her behavior is scented with infantilism. Mostly she tries (until the point of crisis) to keep the right things and the right people in their conventionally right places. So, understanding the behavior of childish, we took its doable nature, lifting it from Nora's circumstances, and transferred it to the circumstances of similar characters that also exhibit the element childish. For example, we put the childishness learned from Nora into the circumstances of Mary Tyrone in O'Neill's *Long Day's Journey into Night*, and then into the circumstances of Blanche DuBois in Williams's *A Streetcar Named Desire*. Although the circumstances of each of these three women differ radically, all three tend to approach their situations childishly. Whether in middle-class Norway, provincial New England, or the French quarter of New Orleans, the behavior of childishness is recognizable as childish. Even though the end of each woman's story differs greatly (Nora is transcending her childishness, Mary is using morphine to return to childhood, and Blanche is being institutionalized because of society's brutality toward childlikeness), they share a main element. Understanding this main element in one character helps the actor approach similar characters.

Similar types exist throughout dramatic literature. They inhabit similar professions and share similar character elements. But the differences in their circumstances make for different plays. No character exists outside a set of given circumstances or a situation. What the character does in response to the given situation reveals who he is. What happens to the character, because of who he is, reveals the theme of the play. Ultimately, the character's element and traits, as well as his aim and actions, are in synchrony with the theme of the play. It is part of the actor's job to help reveal the theme through what he chooses to do as the character and through the manner in which he does it.

To illustrate how knowing the character leads the actor to the theme of a play, Adler selected Peer Gynt, the title role in Ibsen's play. From clues in the script, she ascertained that Peer is a member of the peasant class and a rebel type, evidenced by what he does. Peer disrespects what his mother respects. He scoffs at her Christian morality and ethics. He disobeys her. He pits himself against the religious community. He scorns belief in God, delegating himself his own god. He formulates personal principles of hierarchy and a concept of power. He lies. He steals. He cheats. Peer's rebel type is also evidenced by the reaction of others to what he does. In general, others disparage his actions and attempt to punish him; for example, forbidding him the company of nice girls. Peer's type, therefore, derives from what he is doing most, which is rebelling.

Taking the next step toward developing the character of Peer Gynt, Adler asked, "What does a rebel need?" From indications in the script, it became clear that this rebel needs: godlessness to presume he can create his own life; courage to forge his own trail; arrogance to believe he can blaze the way better than anyone else; strength to assert an individual brand of law and order; exuberance to thrive alone as free as a gypsy; and boldness to want to rebel in the first place. Peer Gynt's rebellion is bold, indicating that a rebel needs boldness. Adler then asked, "What does boldness do?" Again, the script reveals that boldness faces

and surmounts obstacles. Boldness extends itself fully
without fear or needing pity. It springs out and dashes
nonstop, full-speed ahead. It pushes beyond limitations,
and, having panache, it shows off. It is colored brightly
with the traits of brazen, brash, daring, joyful, impudent,
and impertinent. Its colors can be physicalized through
the actions To Joke, To Provoke, To Kid Around. Boldness has keen senses, an alert mind, and a vibrant, flexible
body without tension. Its voice is gleeful. Its speech is
poetic, extraordinary, flamboyant, and articulate. Its language is expansive, stretching beyond logic.

Adler said that with his whole being Peer Gynt bran-
dishes the words "I want what I want. Catch me if you
can." The liveliest of peasants, he is the bold rebel, the
rebel gone overboard, the rebel's rebel. His entire attitude
toward his situation is shaped by immoderation. He is defi-
ant to his mother; and although he does help her it is in his
style, not hers. He is contemptuous of Saint Peter, blocking
him. He is flippant toward Death, making a mockery of
him, as if disallowing even Death to be boring. Since Peer's
rebellion is bold, shattering all the precepts of Christianity,
the play seems to be about what it takes to break the rules,
or about who breaks the rules and how. In this case, the
bold one breaks the rules, going overboard. Accordingly,
through knowing the character, the actor arrives at the
playwright's theme. Thus, all the actor's choices for Peer
Gynt are geared toward activating Ibsen's interest in the
excessive nature of rebellion.

HEIGHTENING CHARACTER

Adler defined heightened character as the type externalized to its theatrical extreme. As in farce or melodrama, it

is characterization so stylized on the outside that the inside can almost be forgotten. Drawn in broad strokes and vividly colored, heightened character requires a rather dualistic perspective. Things are pretty much black and white, not muted or subtle. Heightening takes what Adler called a slanted (biased) view, that results in the type's being theatricalized more than individualized.

The technique for heightening a character is to see him through the eyes of his social opposite, or at least through the eyes of someone radically different. It may be to perceive the servant from the master's viewpoint, the capitalist from the socialist's, the Hollywood starlet from the Christian fundamentalist's, the doctor from the child's, the homosexual from the neo-Nazi's.

Heightening gave us the chance to change everything about ourselves externally almost instantly. The procedure was to select a type, put him in a situation, and portray him physically as his opposite would see him. We took a Japanese military officer, put him in the situation of interrogating a World War II American P.O.W., and portrayed him from the point of view of the boy's mother. Seeing the Japanese through the mother's eyes allowed us to spontaneously change our voice, speech, posture, gestures, and rhythm. Another example was an American Method actor rehearsing the role of Romeo, from the point of view of the British Royal Academy of Dramatic Arts. Adler imagined the Method actor as looking like a slob. He sleeps on a mattress on the floor and wakes up in his jeans at noon, wipes his underarms with a dirty T-shirt, hunts for a cigarette butt in dirty ashtrays, and wielding a broken guitar begins rehearsing his speech to Juliet, saying, "Wherefore? Wherefore what? Wherefore da coffee? Deny yer fadder, dat sonofabitch, deny 'im. Whaddya need 'im for? I always sez yer ole man wazza creep, so deny 'im!" By means of heightening, the actor almost immediately takes on someone he may never have imagined himself becoming.

The principle of heightening is to accept a vision of reality, however biased or illogical, as true. The principle can be applied not only to heightening farcical or melodramatic characters, but also to fantasy or theatre of the absurd characters, in that these plays contain unrealistic or radically heightened circumstances. Adler explained that even though heightened circumstances may break all rules of logic and be downright impossible, the actor uses the circumstances as if they were possible. For example, the actor accepts that he can walk on water, eat the air, or row a boat with straws. But the actor always remains true to the nature of things and of the action, even if the situation is beyond natural. He eats air as air not as meat. He knows that it is air and he believes that air can be eaten—in the circumstances of the play. Or in portraying the Red Queen from *Alice in Wonderland*, who runs and runs and gets nowhere, the actor really does run and run even though she gets nowhere. Thus, with heightening the actor creates a theatrical vision of reality.

Adler referred us to the novels of Charles Dickens to discover a parade of heightened characters; also, to the clown creations of Bert Lahr and Charlie Chaplin to catch the social implications behind heightening. In fact, she said, we could use the social view that heightening takes to influence the external portrayal of any character, even the psychological characters of modern realism. In Adler's opinion, Blanche DuBois from *Streetcar* was already heightened as written, begging to be theatricalized by the actress playing her. Adler considered most of Williams's characters heightened. "He wants them terribly social," she said, "with every moment physicalized." She suggested a background of iced drinks, hot baths, and poetic gentlemen for Blanche, frothy as seen through the brutally practical eyes of Stanley Kowalski. And she suggested building Kowalski as a human beast, as seen through the romantically slanted eyes of Blanche. This socially slanted way of heightening lets each character make a rich social statement on the other. At the same time, it graphically externalizes the play's conflict and helps illuminate the playwright's theme.

Our homework was to watch how people in life switch personality gears to meet their circumstances; how they assume attitudes that automatically heighten their situations socially. Adler illustrated:

> I went to the doctor, and found myself talking to him like this: "Uh, is that going to hurt? I mean, you won't hurt me, will you? No, I'm very comfortable, thank you, thank you very much. Yes, I'm terribly comfortable, and thanks very much for paying so much attention to me." And when I went to say good-bye to the assistant, I said, "Oh, thank you. It was lovely. You really took good care of me. Thank you very much." It was a role. It was a whole role I was playing. I was playing the role of a mouse.

She said that once she recognized that she had given them a show at the doctor's office, she then recognized that she had engaged them in performing for her too. Of course at the time, she had not consciously said to herself, "Hey, I'm a mouse," or "Hey, I'm a polite little girl and you're a big smart man." She had, however, truly viewed and lived the situation as if she were little and the doctor were big.

> Because I did the mouse once, I now know how to do it. The meaning of playing the mouse is that the partner is big and I am little. He knows everything, including how to write with a pencil and read a book. I can say to him, "Gee, isn't that lovely, what a lovely big book!" What results is a very polite, very neat, very tender, very undemanding person— the element of polite from a slanted angle.

Because Adler had created an attitude toward the medical circumstances, a character had emerged and performed a scene. Her commitment to the heightened social view of the character, she recalled, enabled her to play the mouse-meets-authority scene very well. So she said, "What I want you to do, all I want you to do, is play the scene very well." To play any scene very well fundamentally means that the actor believes in an imagined vision of reality.

The Principle is
IN BUILDING A CHARACTER,
LEAVE NOTHING TO CHANCE.

Character According to Society

The actor must have a wide horizon. He will be called upon to present the life of the human spirit of all peoples of the world—present, past, and future.

The actor builds a characterization according to the behavior of the type. The actor defines his acting style according to the behavior of the society with which the play is identified. Early in our training, Adler introduced what she called the "large social classes." These were social groupings based on differences in lifestyle. She wanted us to learn the dominant characteristics typical of each group, including

- Their attitude toward and use of the body.
- Their way of wearing the costume and using properties.
- Their way of thinking and their system of values, including the communal ethics and the religious attitude.
- Their manner of emotional expression.

The idea was to understand the norm of behavior of the social group before even thinking about creating something against the norm. Adler said, "You don't have to understand Picasso, and you don't have to read Dürrenmatt, and you don't have to know who Firbank is. But you do have to know the norm of the social class." Ultimately, she wanted us to be able to physicalize the attitudes of the group—in order to stylize our acting.

We researched and portrayed the behavior of various social classes:

- The Greeks, to reach the psychic size Adler considered necessary for the actor.
- The Clergy, to practice formalized behavior, ritualized movement, and opposing actions.
- The Aristocracy, to develop a substantial sense of self and the use of period costume.
- The Peasantry, to allow for a sense of freedom.
- The Middle Class, to objectively view the norms of our own society, which form the basis of modern drama.

THE GREEKS

Adler explained the fundamental difference between the social ethics of ancient Greek plays and those of today. She said that Greek drama generally comprises characters that represent something greater in magnitude than themselves as individuals. The quest of the Greek protagonist represents the yearning of a collective whole, perhaps the populace of a city. Unlike the modern Western mentality based on a concept of individuality, the Greek mind is conceived by the actor as greater than the individual—not impersonal but larger than personal.

The actor of Greek theatre develops a sense of social responsibility. The acting is presentational, public, opened up and out, and free of tension. "With one thousand people behind and the gods looking on," Adler noted, "there cannot be a struggle in the body. There is an elixir of being, and of being here."

The actor builds the classical body by making every movement intentional and no movement accidental. The gestures are as if they could be sculpted. They are not posed but directed, as in to throw the discus or to drink the hemlock. Greek movement, Adler said, signifies a "readiness to do and die," as if its very need were to idealize the moment.

Adler recommended taking on the attitude of marble to manifest the unified Greek body and mind, since a sculpture made of marble is solid and at ease. The sculpture may lose a hand, a leg, or both arms, but it does not die. Like the Greek warrior, or Keats's "Ode on a Grecian Urn," or the dance of Martha Graham, the essence of marble endures. Marble represents the psychic size of classic plays, the size to which the actor aspires, the size of eternity. It is the same size that Adler identified in the acting of Katharine Cornell:

> Her face was somehow romantic and beautiful, and her acting implied that life goes on inside the play, that she would not die, and that love would not stop. She would not permit the curtain to come down. Her face did not change.

Greek size is accomplished without strain. To develop this ease in size, we worked on physicalizing the character element of power. "Greek power," Adler said, "is the power that does not exert itself: it is the still point of the dance, the opposite of what the Red Queen from *Alice in Wonderland* means when she says, 'It takes all the running you can do to keep in the same place.'" Adler said that the character traits of acuity, arrogance, a sense of justice, and even hatred (activated in scheming) radiate from Greek power.

The whole of the Greek temperament, as Adler conceived it, derives from the expanse of the social tradition, in which the individual is responsible to the populace and accountable to the gods.

Greek temperament is dramatic to the end. A boy might be struck by his father or a girl by her mother, whom she either loves or hates. The rhythm with which the characters live is strike-him-dead rhythm. That rhythm gives the temperament. If there is hatred, it is Greek hate—vengeance by fate: a thousand years of the House of Atreus, plus cursed. The power is built by the actor from the vengeance inside and the relaxation outside. No matter what a character goes through, he does not let the body give way.

The result of a marbleized body and a dramatic temperament, according to Adler, was a face eternalized. Hence the mask of Greek theatre or the mask in the Greek-inspired plays of Eugene O'Neill. Behind the mask is the sense of "I am," which is also identification with one's origins and with the city-state. So for the Greeks, the actor finds a core indestructibility, which stylizes the performance.

Adler suggested we compose ourselves physically, as if girded with steel, and take her advice:

Never mind being small. That's for other people. Don't talk to people who aren't big. Talk to those people who treat you as if you were a queen or a king or a princess. I was brought up that way, and now I don't want to beat around the bush with you. Get marble. You need marble. Marble is a great thing, because it cannot break inside.

Through working on monologues from Greek plays in the

Greek style, we aspired to the experience of belonging to a larger than mundane reality.

THE CLERGY

   To familiarize us with the behavior of the Clergy, Adler showed slides of

- Depictions of Saint Francis of Assisi, for the nature of poverty.
- Paintings by Goya, for the nature of outrage.
- Paintings by Lorenzetti, Simone Martini, Fra Angelico, and the Florentine school of artists, for examples of clerical posture, bearing, and conduct.

Our work was to physicalize traditional images of the Clergy.

   We developed a ritualistic style of behavior, the style of a society of the nonindustrialized Middle Ages, when the Church was sovereign; a society whose way of thinking was based on a concept of right and wrong, saint and sinner—or spirit and body. We examined the mind of the Clergy so as to clarify the Clergy's action and movement. We discovered that when the social values are clearly black and white, there is no gray ground, no halfway sea of indeterminacy in which to float. We came to understand the nature of action motivated by a need to perpetuate a belief in God. We came to experience the nature of toil performed in a spirit of reverence, and the nature of security founded on a feeling of alignment with God.

   Adler instructed us to think of the Clergy body as a vehicle for performing ceremony. Concealed beneath gowns, it is asexual, in repose, and almost silent. We dressed in clerical costume to experience its refining effect on the body. We walked in procession, knelt, stretched toward heaven, and prayed in unison. Adler posed questions:

> Wearing these clothes, do you see how easily you can live without pockets? Wearing these clothes, could you ever think of leaning on a chair? Is it ever necessary to look for the chair before sitting down? Is your aim in sitting not bigger than To Sit? Are you not sitting in order To Hear or To Witness something? When you believe "Dust thou art and to dust thou shalt return," are you not secure? Is the floor no longer the floor? Is it not the earth?

We studied the action To Suppress as a primary aim for the Clergy; specifically, to suppress personal inclinations in order to serve the Church. Adler presented an image of the Pietà, created, she said, to depict the concealment of profound suffering. She described suppression as a religious trait, activated by containing oneself, holding back impulses, and checking feelings. We also activated its opposite, To Release, which we imagined, in keeping with the clerical code, would be done in private; for example, self-flagellation in one's cell.

We learned that when the values of a society are clearly defined (as they are not in modern society), movement is more formal and gesture more deliberate. Action is strictly under control or is its dramatic opposite, as in righteous indignation. Unlike the modern character in a struggle for identity, the Clergy consciousness is communal and mutually understood.

THE ARISTOCRACY

In Adler's assessment, the United States lacks an aristocratic tradition, except for a kind of spiritual aristocracy peopled by artists of all disciplines. She looked to paintings of seventeenth-century French court life and the art of Velázquez and Goya to exemplify the society of the aristocrat, which she contrasted to the society of the Greeks and of the Clergy in terms of their way of thinking about themselves.

Like a member of the Clergy (from which the Aristocracy inherits its rituals of behavior), the aristocrat is able to believe "I am here by the grace of God." Unlike a member of the Clergy, however, the aristocrat gives importance to his or her body. The aristocrat's entire direction is toward the self, supported by his or her elevated social status and tradition of bloodlines. While the priest acts as a servant of God and His people, and the Greek acts as a representative of the people, the aristocrat dominates the people.

Adler instructed us to arrange the circumstances of the aristocrat so as to present ourselves as important and large. We chose materials for the aristocrat based on creating an attitude of superiority and decorating oneself. The costume was to make us appear big, deserving of access to palatial space. To reach the physicality typical of the Aristocracy, the actor fundamentally obeys the costume, resulting in sparse gesture and movement.

We differentiated the world of the Aristocracy from the world of the Middle Class. We discovered that To Wield Power, rather than To Acquire Material, is the main aim of the Aristocracy. The power is ruling power, impersonal and uninvolved; as Adler noted, it can be found in the scenes of warfare, coronation, and ceremony in Shakespeare's history plays. With the Aristocracy, the actor experiences a society not suffering from Middle Class alienation, but a society assuming that God is on its side and the people are under its control.

THE PEASANTRY

Adler took characteristics for the Peasantry from the works of painters like Breughel and van Gogh. Our purpose in rehearsing peasant behavior was to be liberated from physical inhibition, ritualized behavior, and analytical thinking. Adler was not so interested in having us characterize a peasant character from literature. She wanted us to experience the nature of peasant life, particularly in contrast to the nature of Middle Class life.

The culture of the peasant begins and ends with the earth. "He [in contrast to the Gypsy or the migrant worker] is not a wanderer on the land. He is part of the land," Adler said. His entire existence is connected to Nature. She pointed out how, in Breughel paintings, the mud of the path is tracked indoors onto the floor, while the contents of the house spill outdoors onto the path. The Peasantry stay rooted to the earth to which they and their effects belong. They dig potatoes in rough and rocky ground, wash themselves in the same stream they drink from, eat with their hands the food they have grown, drink their homemade wine from a skin sack, build a table from the trees around them, and sleep on a dirt or wooden floor.

The society of the Peasantry is based on a communal way of life. The people are neither alone nor lonely, but are unified through a shared purpose. Therefore, when the actor performs peasant tasks, he acts without prejudice, unbiased toward age or gender. The peasant is unified with the group through physical contact. Touching is not peripheral. There is no shame and nothing to hide. Babies are openly fed at the breast. Everything, including peasants' sexuality, is as exposed and robust as among the animals they tend. This naturalness of the Peasantry, Adler said, was absolutely unknown to us.

> It is not within your education. It is not within what you have seen. Individually, you might have had a drunken night; but [within the Peasantry] sexy, masculine men have unsentimental fun partying, dancing, and mating with earthy women. Everybody is a somebody familiar, to whom you do not have to say hello. The body is normal, very much of a whole, like the potato.

To physicalize the peasant attitude toward the body, Adler advised us to "take out the whole Middle Class." But, she added, "It is not the body of a slob. . . in an American way. It is all of a piece, not divided and not needing a chair to hold it up. The body sits unconstrained, as rude as the stool it's spread upon." We discovered in portraying the Peasantry that the body is made rough and heavy by work; that it is a primitive body, whose movement is organic, and when at rest or asleep, it is abandoned.

In respect of the peasant mentality, Adler offered her memory of what Stanislavsky had said.

> I know how to play a peasant. I know how he wipes his nose. I know everything about him. But I don't know, when he stands for four hours, what he is thinking. I know what I think, and I know what my

friends think, and what an actor thinks, and what
[Ibsen's] Brand thinks, and what many other people think, but I don't know what he thinks.

Adler contended that peasants do not think, except in
images. Everything of the peasant mind, she said, is singular
and simple. When she gave us the simple physical action To
Count Potatoes, she suggested making it tedious. "But,"
she said, "don't play an idiot. The peasant is smart as hell."
She taught us to use our imagination to respond to the
sources of peasant language. She wanted us to speak only
basic words: baby, fire, death, fun, food. Any new word was
a puzzle to be solved through experience. So, we found that
the peasant may learn the meaning of punishment through
a beating with a stick, the meaning of sleep through falling down dog-tired, the meaning of work through being
rewarded with something to eat. We were not to try to
make sense with words, but to speak through action. When
portraying the peasant, Adler said, the actor does not need
English or the language of a particular nation. Rather, she
said, the actor needs a kind of gibberish understood by his
peasant group with its absolute oneness of thought.

Because of their contact with Nature, as we experienced,
the Peasantry radiates an unself-conscious spirituality.
Having all their truth at hand, they are stable and secure.
Unlike the Middle Class, the Peasantry does not know anxiety. Although the features of the peasant may sometimes
appear coarse or distorted, the peasant face is most often
depicted as vigorous, robustly charming, never romantically
soft. The peasant is graphic. The peasant is overt. But the
peasant, Adler insisted, is not the farmer. The true peasant is someone, she said, who nobody limited to North

America has ever seen. In embodying the characteristics of the Peasantry, we were free to rid ourselves of everything in our backgrounds inappropriate to a society whose values are not in a state of conflict.

THE MIDDLE CLASS

Adler used photographs from *Life* magazine to examine images of the Middle Class. She traced the growth and development of the Middle Class to the rise of industrialization and a dependence upon machinery in daily life. Since Middle Class values and conduct fuel the issues of modern drama, understanding the norm of the class is the actor's imperative.

In Adler's view, the Middle Class is void of the communal sensibility that coheres in the Peasantry, the Clergy, and the Greeks. It is a class divided, riveted in states of conflict between husbands and wives, parents and children, and political platforms. Conflict erupts because the Middle Class lacks a firm, steady, binding ethical ideal. The class has produced no mythology (as with the Greeks), no king (as with the Aristocracy), no God (as with the Clergy), and no real contact with Nature (as with the Peasantry) to provide a shared world-view or system of morality. Though composed of a nonrebellious people, the Middle Class sustains a permanent condition of rebellion within itself: members against members and members against the current standard of how things ought to be. As a result, members are alienated from one another. Only when uniting behind a social, economic, or political cause do they connect.

Adler used the Middle Class to demonstrate how the mentality of a group influences the attitude toward the body. She said that when a person's body is not organically joined to the earth (Peasantry), or is not the temple of the soul (Clergy), or neither represents the people (Greeks) nor controls them (Aristocracy), it is a shell. We physicalized the Middle Class body as constrained, revealing that the human tradition of being connected to one's body had been lost. Likewise, we discovered that the spiritual tradition of being connected to one's soul had also been lost.

Like the Middle Class body, the Middle Class house, possessions, and emotions are kept under control. In fact, Adler said, the predominant feature of Middle Class society is orderliness. The purpose of this arrangement is twofold: to impress others and to conceal the truth. To be concerned about what others think, in contrast to the Aristocracy's indifference toward opinion, is a Middle Class obligation. Adler referred to the Middle Class way of thinking as "the institution of 'I believe,'" by which she meant the ability to appropriate what one is told without experiencing it. She saw the Middle Class way of thinking as organized, and the overall attitude, created from accepting what the newspapers print, as institutional.

We imagined the typical Middle Class person as someone living a family life, whose ideas, morals, and values are supplied respectively by his government, religious organization, and economic situation. The Middle Class person has no need to change the world. Since the activities of his daily life are familiar and the people around are recognizable, he is at home and at ease in a pleasant place, that is actually made pleasant by the institutions which he follows.

Given this base, we recognized how conflict or drama arises. When the Middle Class son dates a chorus girl or when the executive grows long hair or when the daughter brings home a bohemian, domestic conflict arises over standards or values. The conflict that occurs between the husband and wife when he grows long hair, Adler pointed out, arises not because of her own disliking his hair but because the institutions dislike long hair. Middle Class conflict is the result of group thinking being challenged by personal thinking. In this sense, Ibsen's *Ghosts*, in Adler's view, was a great Middle Class play, because Mrs. Alving reveals the conflict (as well as suffering and turmoil) brought about by institutionally enforced thinking.

We learned that Middle Class society expects a Middle Class character to use the circumstances logically. The expectation for a chair is something upon which to sit, not upon which to fling one's feet. Furthermore, the Middle Class, in wanting things to be logical, gives importance to facts. There is a hesitancy to penetrate the depths of another person, or to expose oneself in communication. Generally, more is said than is believed or felt. Adler explained that in the works of such playwrights as Ibsen, Strindberg, Shaw, Williams, Miller, Albee, and Neil Simon, the actor must look for the mainstay of Middle Class life, which is the social performance of human deportment. Portraying a Middle Class character involves experiencing the pretense of Middle Class social and domestic life. It is the pretense that stylizes the acting.

Just as we had learned that the actor establishes the type until the play's social situation reveals the individual, so too we learned that the actor establishes the conventions of the society until the play's social situation reveals the unconventional. Until Nora in *A Doll's House* challenges the standard role of woman within the institution of marriage, her domestic life conforms to Middle Class expectations.

With the study of each society, we found general

expectations regarding behavior. Each society has its norm and standards, due to some level of commonality in the members' approach to life. The actor needs to understand the norm and standards, or the rules of the society depicted in the play. The rules indicate the acting style and stabilize the actor's performance. The actor measures the choices of his character against the rules. Revealing the individual within the society, the actor/character follows the rules or breaks them.

The Principle is
EVERYONE EXISTS WITHIN A SOCIETY AND IS INFLUENCED BY ITS LIFE.

Chapter V

Text: What the Actor Knows

The play is the social situation and its inherent conflict.

When an actor first approaches a play, the script is an alien thing. Woven of words not of his choosing, peopled with strangers, marked with events he has not experienced and situations he has not unexplored, the play stands all in shadow. The actor infuses the play with the light of life. Reading the words of a play, the actor systematically works backward from the words to the sources of the play and then works forward to speak the words—simply and meaningfully. It is a creative research process, to find what he can use to fill the text with as much insight, thought, and imagination as was stirring in the playwright before he arrived at the result of all his labor—the result being: the words.

Adler taught that the actor first reads the play to uncover the plot—what happens in the story. He notes the sequences of action: How does the play build?—and he notes the direction of each sequence: Does the sequence build up or down? He commits a summary of the sequences to memory, as if in response to someone's saying "I've never read this story or seen it on the stage. Tell me what it's about." The actor does not memorize words.

The actor then reads his part aloud, allowing whatever sense he finds in the text to emerge. The actor does not impose anything on the text. He does not act or even interpret. He simply sees what is there to understand. At the same time, he discovers the energy level of the play, which is influenced by whether the lines are in verse or prose and the tone is light or dark. Getting the energy level stylizes the reading, coloring it more vibrantly than beige. In reading aloud, the actor also looks for any conflict or misunderstanding between characters and accentuates that tension. This way, the actor immediately gets the play's conflict of values agitating within his own breast.

If not in a second reading then in a third, the actor writes down impressions, scene by scene, having to do with:

- The atmosphere or mood of each scene.
- Who his character is.
- Whom his character is with.
- The place where his character is.
- The time period and society of the play.

He then traces these impressions back to specific lines, that is, to statements of fact within the text. In this way he solidifies the play's social situation and verifies it. As Adler said, "If you do not know the social situation, you will not know how to act." It is through understanding, expanding on, and internalizing the social situation that the actor is able to realize the text.

THE SOCIAL SITUATION AND THE CONFLICT OF THE PLAY: The social situation definitively affects a character's behavior. Adler related an experience of finding herself in the company of an American doctor and his spouse, a former member of the Nazi youth movement. In that circumstance, Adler was prompted to announce, "Either she leaves this room or I do." Understanding the social situation tells the actor what attitude to assume toward the partner and what to do about him or her.

The actor states the social situation, as he has come to know it from the facts of the play, in the present tense. This immediacy gives him a springboard into studying, thinking about, and imagining the way of life of the society that determined the play's social situation. The words or facts of a script are there to stimulate the actor to think. They help him construct a whole background for the play, including the society's way of thinking. Specifically, the actor needs to be concerned with what the society of the play thinks, in terms of

- Politics, or the distribution and use of power.
- Economics, or the distribution and use of money.
- Sociology, or the class structure and acceptable behavior in public (including the attitude toward minorities).
- Domesticity, or the family structure and acceptable behavior in the home (including the attitude toward women).
- Religion, or the system of beliefs, morals, and practices.

Referring to the text and using imagination, the actor gradually develops this background, giving it body. He seeks out literature and works of art from the time period and locale where the play is set. He immerses himself in images typical of the play's social class. Thus rich with a wealth of attitudes appropriate to the social situation of the play, he fulfills one job of the actor: to figure out how to live and react within the given code.

According to what Adler taught, the play is essentially the social situation and its inherent conflict. In the modern theatre, the play is contained within the place and may be acted because of the place. To illustrate, Adler asked us to consider the circumstances of a hospital. We needed to immediately understand that a hospital implies a rhythm, a logical nature, a sense of purpose, and a way of doing and being that are different from ours. The actor gets the differences between the world of the play and his everyday life by gathering impressions from the text. For example, the text of Sidney Kingsley's *Men in White*, which is set in a hospital, not only tells the actor the facts—the time of day, the season, the country, and the century—but it also indicates the nature of the immediate circumstances and the behavior required to live in those circumstances.

Adler gathered impressions from *Men in White* to analyze the circumstances of a hospital. She defined it as a place insulated from the regular world and full of activities generally incomprehensible to outsiders. She noted a separation between the staff and the patients, and concluded that each group is imprisoned within the place and that neither is free to act personally. The staff, a hierarchy of people in uniform, practices nonintimate behavior toward the patients and each other. When something personal enters the scene—for example, when a kiss surreptitiously occurs between a doctor and a nurse—the pattern of formality is broken. Conflict potentially arises and drama (or comedy) ensues. Any behavior against the formalized nature of the hospital place, including against the nature of the starched, white, unadorned nurse's uniform/costume, indicates individuality within the medical-profession type. The social situation pushes the kiss into high relief. The kiss becomes unsterile, disorderly, personal behavior in a sterile, orderly, impersonal place, between otherwise professional people. The actors, therefore, affected by their knowledge of the circumstances, bring to the kiss an attitude toward what they are doing in the place. Through the kiss, the actors reveal the conflict in the social situation; that is, they create the play.

THE CHARACTER'S MAIN AIM AND THE PLAYWRIGHT'S THEME: The actor approaches the character through the commonality of the type. First, the actor discovers the differences between himself and the type. The actor narrows down the type to a character with a name. For example, the character might be an artist type in modern times, specifically a film actress, namely Meryl Streep the individual. Consulting the play, the actor discovers how the individual lives in accord with, or against, the type; in particular, how the individual manages within her society: what she does and where she likes to go in her daily round. The actor imaginatively creates an entire background for the character, built out of the facts and impressions of the text. Thus, the actor nails the type and the play reveals the individual.

Next, the actor seeks to discover the character's aim, which is what the character wishes to accomplish most in life. The actor has to have identified the playwright's theme—which is the main idea of the play, spoken through the social situation—in order to figure out the character's aim, since the actor determines the aim in relation to the theme. When the actor has determined the character's aim, he checks the validity of all the actions he selects for the character against this aim, since all the character's actions need to go toward fulfilling the character's aim—whether that aim is ever actually fulfilled in the play or not. Thus, the actor as character helps reveal the theme of the play through the action he individually takes in response to the circumstances. Or, the actor/character's aim is his specific answer to the overall social situation.

Adler noted that it is often difficult to pinpoint a character's aim and that the actor might conceivably take a wrong direction. But when the actor does find the right aim for his character and ties all his actions to this aim, his acting spotlights the big ideas of the play. Arriving at the aim, or super-objective, of the character, Adler said, is the very center of the Stanislavsky System.

To find the character's aim, the actor returns to the text. The words get him thinking about what needs to be accomplished in the circumstances. For example, taking Konstantin in Chekhov's *The Sea Gull*, Adler gathered the impression that Konstantin is burdened with an apprehensive streak, based on the comments of other characters concerning his nostalgia and depression. Such clues were Adler's key to Konstantin's possible aim being To Resolve My Feelings of Apprehension. She selected this aim in respect of Chekhov's theme; that is, an exploration of the artist's need for faith in order to survive. The actor directs all of Konstantin's undertakings—his writing, his attentions to Nina, his seeking the love of his mother—toward resolving his apprehension or lack of faith. In the end, the obstacles to Konstantin's winning his aim are too great to overcome. His nostalgia and depression (or his lack of faith) overpower his aim. Even as Konstantin loses his aim in an act of suicide, the actor playing the part enriches Chekhov's theme.

Especially with modern plays, according to Adler, the actor has to understand and physicalize the complexities of the character's psychology. The actor is not onstage to relate the plot but to activate the character's aim. The actor can safely activate the character's aim insofar as he directs the doing of every physical action, verbal action, and inner action toward the character's aim. In fact, all the actor can do is play one action after another toward an aim. He cannot play emotions, or a characterization, or images, or an atmosphere. Those are unplayable, or not doable, until they are translated into action or made doable. Adler recalled that when a Moscow Art Theatre actor portraying Romeo described the character's action as to be hopelessly in love, Stanislavsky corrected his language by saying that Romeo's action is To Hopelessly Pay Attention to Juliet. To be in love is a condition, not an action. A condition is not playable. To Pay Attention to is an action. Only an action is playable.

The actor does not stand around in a scenic atmosphere. The actor discovers what he can do in the circumstances, and the doing evokes an atmosphere. The actor reflects on the play's circumstances before entering the stage and thinks while onstage. He finds thoughts that excite and agitate him; for example, thoughts of Romeo in relation to Juliet in their social situation, or thoughts of Konstantin in relation to Nina in their social situation. What the actor thinks about as Romeo enables him to pay attention to Juliet hopelessly, evoking an atmosphere of love. These enabling thoughts can come only from the actor; they cannot be imparted by the director, since, as Adler said, "The director does not know what thoughts inspire the actor."

As Adler explained, by thinking about the character's circumstances and his or her aim (what the character needs to accomplish), the actor develops feelings for the character. When the actor plays within a context of understanding, he awakens his emotions, and sensations well up within. Then the actor believes in the reality of his work.

The actor's artistic goal is to have faith in what he is doing. The actor gets that faith from knowing the life behind the words. To act without this knowledge, which is to act without confidence, is to go onstage and die. Faith, Adler said, is the lesson all artists may learn from Konstantin, who died from a lack of faith in his work.

THE LIFE BEHIND THE LINES: Everything that Adler taught was aimed at helping the actor create the play. All the technique she offered was to help the actor discover what he needs to put behind the lines of the text, moment to moment, sequence to sequence, to create the play. When the actor believes in the life behind the lines, he is free to think and do and feel on the stage. He is able to live the life of a real person in a real place, over and over again, and not redundantly.

To get us thinking about the life behind the lines, Adler analyzed a section of Philip Barry's *Hotel Universe*; specifically, a sequence between the characters Ann Field and Pat Farley. Her analysis included a summary of the actor's procedure and principles when facing a text.

So, the actor reads the play. He defines the plot, and then the sequences, including how the sequences build, up or down. The actor reads through the text again, gathering impressions. For example, with the sequence from *Hotel Universe*, Adler listed her impressions as

- There is a feeling of love between them.
- Ann is concerned about Pat.
- Pat knows what is important in life but pretends not to know.
- Even though Pat may love Ann, he is thinking of something else, and what he is thinking of is more compelling to him just now than loving her.
- They are of the Middle Class, so family life is important to both of them.

SEE WHAT IS THERE.
DO NOT IMPOSE UPON THE SCRIPT.

Next, the actor reads the scene aloud, letting whatever he thinks come out of the play. He does not read into the script, does not act the script, and does not make the reading colorless. Through reading, something happens; also, some conflict emerges. The actor looks for the conflict and intensifies it, or, as Adler said, "agitates" it.

WHEN READING, IMMEDIATELY SEE
THROUGH YOUR IMAGINATION.

The actor begins to build up a background for the larger circumstances. He notes the setting and asks questions. For example, as applied to *Hotel Universe*, Adler said to look into the following:

- *The Period*—The play is set in 1929, before the Great Depression. What is the morality and what is the social behavior of the Middle Class at the time?
- *The Society*—The play depicts Upper Middle Class life. The characters do not speak poetically, but Middle

Class colloquially. Their speech gives the acting style.
- *The Characters*—What is each one's nationality? Class? Costume? How does each one announce himself socially? What are three problems the character and partner have shared, and how was each problem solved? What are some personal things they have revealed to each other?

YOU MUST DE-FICTIONALIZE THE FICTION BY ACTIVATING THE PAST.

The actor builds up a background for the immediate circumstances. He notes the facts and begins to build upon the facts imaginatively. Adler gave instructions:

- *The Partner*—Write out his or her history and build your relationship. When and where did you meet? Why did you like each other? What has happened in his or her life? You must have the ability to have a relationship with your partner in three or four different sets of circumstances, each of which you justify. Select justification that is toward, not away from, your action. Select justification that comes quickly from behind the lines and makes you respond. Your talent lies in your choice of justification. There is nothing to push, there is nothing to sell, especially in realistic theatre.
- *The Set*—Make a drawing of the set. You cannot do an action unless you are in some place. First place yourself. Then use the stage physically with ease before going to the lines. Be able to live alone in the set.
- *The Action*—What is your action, sequence by sequence? Physicalize as much as possible. It is better to use your

body than to speak words. Begin with simple physical actions in the place, doing one action after another truthfully, several times. In the beginning, do many simple physical actions. Do more physical actions in the place than you will ever need. Later, you can select.

GET USED TO PRESENTING AN ILLUSION OF TRUTH.

The actor returns to the text. He plays the actions, one by one, toward the character's aim. For example, with *Hotel Universe*, Adler determined that Ann's action when she enters the scene is To Fight Him Back Point by Point, with an aim to become his equal. The actress physicalizes the action: At Ann's entrance, Adler said, the actress has to do something to get herself onstage and into the situation. She has to give herself something to ignite the action. For example, she can come on and tear up a letter. She must not come on and announce herself with an entrance line. She must come on doing something that helps her say her entrance line, so that the line comes out of what she is doing. So, according to Adler's vision, Ann's role in the scene may go as follows:

Ann enters and tears up a letter as she says, "I won't have it, Pat, I just will not have it." She stays away from him.

Pat says, "It? What's that you won't have?"

She picks up a half-empty bottle of whiskey. Looking at the bottle, thinking thoughts, she brings her next line out of what she is thinking: "Something's burning you up. Tell me what it is!" She goes to him.

He says, "I'm afraid you're imagining things." His action, in response to what the partner is doing, is To Cool It.

IF YOU CAN DO THREE MINUTES,
YOU CAN DO A WHOLE PLAY.

The actor makes a contribution. He refines his tools, replenishes his resources, and uses the techniques. Since the actor's profession is acting, his contribution is through the play. Since the human being is the subject of the play, and the playwright's theme is the object of the play, the actor as character is responsible for revealing the theme of the play. Through what he chooses to do onstage, the actor reveals the theme. He physicalizes his understanding of the theme, making it clear to the audience so it may touch their lives. This is the vocation of the actor.

Adler offered assistance to fulfill the actor's vocation. She presented a series of what she called extensions, ways for the actor to extend the play from the page to the stage.

THE EXTENSIONS OF THE PLAY:

1. UNDERSTAND YOURSELF
AND YOUR SOCIETY.

Give up your mask and masked ideas of yourself. Be able to answer the question "Who am I?" Answer this question in relation to life in modern society, which has to do with the fact that everyone wants to get the most out of life. How do you get the most out of life in a world of difficulties and problems? Know your aim in your own life and the price you are willing to pay for that aim.

Know your society. None of us exists outside of a place

and its society. In terms of modern society, we are basically out of balance and uncentered, being pushed and pulled by societal expectations. Know yourself in relation to the conditions of our society.

Once you determine who you are, ask yourself, "What is the opposite? Where have I seen this opposite in the world and in myself?" The answers will help you know yourself even better, and will enable you to play both sides of an idea relating to a theme.

2. UNDERSTAND THE DIFFERENCE BETWEEN YOURSELF AND THE CHARACTER.

From knowledge and intuition, discover the differences between the way you think and the way the charac-ter thinks. Know the character in relation to two basic directions of humankind: 1) to live for the satisfaction of appetites; and 2) to struggle for something higher than appetite gratification by striving to give oneself. (The theme of most modern plays involves the conflict between these two basic directions and the price of each. The price of the first direction is self-destruction. The price of the second direction is self-sacrifice.) Keep these contrasting directions in mind when building a background for the circumstances and the character.

Determine what price your character is willing to pay for the direction he chooses. Therefore, know his aim. Ask yourself, "What does my character hope for? Where does his life want to go? What price has he already paid for becoming who he has wanted to become?"

After determining your character's aim, figure out his

attitude toward everything and everyone in the play. Recognize how his struggle within himself or his conflict with
the partner derives from his attitudes.

Use justification to become fully on the side of your
character, giving birth to how he thinks and feels—different
from how you think and feel. Get to the role through the
character's attitudes and thoughts, and through justification of his attitudes in relation to the theme. Let the words
of the play affect you as a character with specific attitudes.
Realize that no role is you, but you are in every role.

3. UNDERSTAND THE PARTNER, IN RELATION TO YOUR CHARACTER.

Know the partner from what he does, from his attitude
toward the place, from his use of the props and the
immediate circumstances, and from what you perceive
to be behind his words. Hear what the partner is saying
underneath the lines.

Determine your attitude toward the partner—how you
estimate him—by comparing his way of life to your character's way of life in relation to the theme. Include your
understanding of the partner's relationship to the theme
(therefore, his aim) in the way you speak and respond to
him. (In general, the partner is for or against the values of
the society and is a success or a failure—in relation to the
theme.) See how the theme affects the partner (indeed,
every character in the play). The theme is the spine of the
play, or what the play is exploring.

Recognize that your character exists only because he is
related to the theme. Understand your character in relation to the partner's relationship to the theme. Let your

character's internal life evolve onstage during the performance, in consideration of the internal life of the partner. In other words, decide in the moment what to put behind your lines in consideration of what the partner is putting behind his lines.

4. REVEAL YOUR UNDERSTANDING OF THE THEME IN YOURSELF THROUGH WHAT YOU DO ONSTAGE.

Remember that the audience understands your character not so much through the ideas you speak but through what you do. Let the audience *see* who your character is, and understand what his aim is, in relation to the theme.

What you choose to do onstage is important. Do not just do what you feel like doing. Do not just be busy. Make thoughtful choices regarding how you handle your props and materials—all according to the place and its effect on your character.

Make your choices in the direction of the theme, so your acting lifts the play. Figure out the crisis of the play. Broach this crisis or conflict. Get involved in the modern dilemma. Ask yourself, "How do I as the character find a solution as to how to live? How might my solution be different from the solutions of others, even though I am a human being in the same struggle as everyone else?" What you choose to do onstage reveals your understanding of the theme.

Return to the technique that keeps you truthful. Let your truthfulness talk to the audience. Let your humanity speak through you, the actor acting, not through the words.

Through practicing these four extensions of the play, the

actor elevates the profession of acting. Using his craft, the actor enacts, not simply states, the conflict of ideas and the resolution of drama. In a sense, the actor is a medium for audience insight and human harmony. In public, onstage, the actor uses himself to create the nature of a human being and to explore the nature of the human condition. Ultimately, perhaps, since what exists onstage in the modern theatre is the actor revealing his understanding of the theme, it is the actor that is the play.

Adler said, "The actor has a very big job." Most of the actor's work, in Adler's opinion, lay in thinking about the play—realizing the four extensions. According to his understanding of the play, the actor discovers his contribution.

> The actor who is a real actor will ask, "What can I give the play? What can I contribute? What truth can I find and reveal?" The dividend for him is a growth in self-revelation. That growth comes through this work of understanding, which helps him become what he wants to become—the artist/ human being.

Adler's ethic for the actor, then, was essentially the same ethic that Stanislavsky evolved. As Adler put it, "Have the discipline to love the art in yourself, rather than yourself in the art."

The Principle is
YOUR BIGGEST CONTRIBUTION IS
TO FIND THE SELF YOU DID NOT KNOW.

CHAPTER VI

The Development of the Artist–Human Being

Let it not be forgotten that Stella Adler was the only American to have studied with Constantine Stanislavsky, maker of modern acting; indeed, Stanislavsky worked with Stella Adler directly one-on-one for five weeks in Paris in 1934. On returning from Paris to New York City, she offered classes to the actors of the Group Theatre, sharing her lessons learned. Essentially, she cut through the confusion around the System as it had been interpreted stateside in the early 1930s. American actors to this day benefit from Stella's five weeks with Stanislavsky, especially in how she clarified and built upon his System; and from the whole of her life in the theatre. She was raised by prodigiously talented parents, Jacob and Sara Adler, monarchs of the Yiddish Theatre; established a legitimate stage presence in the 1920s and '30s; was a featured player in three Hollywood studio movies; and built a forty-two-year teaching career untainted by commercialism. Stella earned her reputation of prominence as a teacher.

Elia Kazan, Sanford Meisner, and Robert Lewis were among Stella's first pupils in the Group Theatre. She offered them a creative perspective that, by their own admissions, affected their ways of working with actors thereafter. At the New School in New York City in the 1940s, she taught Marlon Brando, who went on to change film acting entirely, not least by his transfiguration of the male body on screen. (I recall Arthur Miller saying that at the December 1947 opening of *A Streetcar Named Desire*, when Brando took off his shirt, women in the audience fainted.) At her own New York studio, founded in 1949, she taught Robert De Niro. In the late 1960s she headed the acting program at Yale, where her former pupil and Yale successor, Bobby Lewis, taught Meryl Streep. In Los Angeles, she taught Benicio del Toro and Mark Ruffalo. She taught Kate Valk, who joined the Wooster Group, and Kate Mulgrew, who joined *Star Trek*. She taught hundreds, and among them were some of the few that most actors look to for how acting is done.

The five master acting teachers of the twentieth century were all connected to the Group Theatre—Lee Strasberg, Sanford Meisner, and Robert Lewis, along with Stella, as Group members; and Uta Hagen, who excelled as an actor under the direction and tutelage of Harold Clurman. (Clurman was co-founder of the Group Theatre and was married to Stella Adler from 1943 to 1960. He was also my professor turned friend from 1968 until his death in 1980.) As noted by Stella's grandson Tom Oppenheim, Artistic Director of the Stella Adler Studio for Acting in New York, if Lee Strasberg was the first American to apply an aspect of the Stanislavsky System to making American theatre, then Stella Adler was the first American to diversify Stanislavsky's methodology.

Stella Adler did not make use of Lee Strasberg's term "The Method." She called what she offered a grabbable, doable, human nature–based "Technique" of acting, applicable universally to all forms of theatre and styles of acting. The teaching approaches of Lee Strasberg and Stella Adler were in conflict. The differences between them were whether to use affective memory or imagination: which comes first, emotion or action? Strasberg instructed actors to recall their own past events as a way of resurrecting emotions needed to play a scene, asserting that feeling leads to acting. Adler rejected Strasberg's emphasis on the actors bringing personal experience into the given circumstances of a play. She instructed actors to play an action, asserting that feelings would follow. I recall Harold Clurman mentioning that Lee Strasberg, whom he held like a brother, was an emotionally reticent person, given to difficulty expressing his feelings. Clurman surmised that Strasberg's method of eliciting an actor's emotions was a means of expression *for him*. Squeezing out the emotion, as Stella called it, was tantamount to illness. In a letter to me in 1985, she wrote, "I know that the Strasberg cancer will go on and on and on . . . and even when it is physically curable. It's a kind of road that occurs in life—the wrong track. It can build generations of cripples." Stella's lament echoed her storied quote that it would take decades for American acting to recover from Strasberg. The phrase, as I originally heard it, was that it would take "fifty years" after Strasberg's death, which puts us in 2032, not impossibly far into the future, when it shall at last be time for their variances to dissolve!

Stella Adler gave the world of performing arts a way of sanity for the actor, resulting in the actor's *independence* from the teacher; the ability to work *interdependently* with fellow actors and the mind of the playwright; and the ability to work *nondependently* with the director. Her way of sanity focused on mastering a craft which entailed: 1) learning how to build a truthful performance in any style of play-writing—that's the material component; and 2) pursuing total growth as a human being by virtue of figuring out not only how to be a better person, a la Stanislavsky, but how to live a noble life—that's the spiritual component. As aphorized by Stella's grandson Tom Oppenheim, "Growth as an actor and growth as a human being are synonymous."

Among the twentieth-century masters, Stella comes out most trustworthy, according to Rose Malague in her unique and carefully researched book *An Actress Prepares*. (Rose, who was my student in graduate school, now holds a faculty position in Theatre Arts at the University of Pennsylvania.) As Malague attests, Stella was exemplary not only in terms of what she taught but also in how she related to students. Yes, Stella was strict and relentless when it came to assessing students' work; she was nevertheless respectful, meeting students "without sexual predation, intentional intimidation, or psychological domination."

Stella Adler's Technique, as described in the five previous chapters of this book, is apparently neither fully nor widely taught across America today. In her lifetime Stella didn't attempt to expand her influence by pushing students into stardom—she was not a fame-monger—or by anointing teachers to carry on her legacy. I remember her saying that an acting studio, or a system of acting, is not the material of a franchise.

I'd like to propose Stella Adler, a unique bearer of sanity, as a figure of unity among the master acting teachers of the twentieth century and their descendants. She embraced, and moved beyond, the lineage of Stanislavsky. She opened a door. There after, all manner of caring people invented all sorts of acting exercises, allowing an "amalgamation of teachings" to emerge. Today's teachers of acting, using the amalgamation, may invoke Sandy Meisner's exercises for freeing up a student's instincts and unblocking his impulses; or they may invoke The Method; and so on. Their aim is to produce the ideal actor; in fact, says Malague, today's amalgamation of exercise-based teachings doesn't add anything significant to the essence and spirit of what Stella taught. It seems to me that Stella Adler, in one way or another, pointed out just about everything an actor may need to take charge of his own artistic achievement. And that is precisely the sense in which she may be considered a figure of unity. I warrant, if Adler's Technique were fully and widely taught in studios of acting and academic theatre programs going forward, it would transform American acting from self-centered to selflessly sacred.

Through a process of reexamining the teachings of Stella Adler, I've landed upon a blueprint that brings her uniqueness up to date. The blueprint lays out a lifelong path for the actor, culminating in the development of the Artist–Human Being. The way of the actor's path is the quintessence of this new chapter for the new edition.

TEACHER–HUMAN BEING

Before presenting the blueprint, I want to sketch for you, especially the young reader, the personality of Stella Adler, beyond what appears in the "Introduction" chapter of this book, that you may conjure the astonishing aliveness she radiated, apparently to her dying day. Harold Clurman introduced me to Stella Adler at the Broadway opening in December 1968 of Tyrone Guthrie's *The House of Atreus.* My first glimpse of her in the role of teacher was

in September 1969 as per the description of my classmate
Jeanne Hall: "We're all seated in the Studio, we're all ner-
vous—it's the first day of class—we're waiting, and we're
waiting, and waiting, and waiting, and the door swings
open, and Stella walks in a few steps. She lifts one arm over-
head and then she flings the other arm upward and throws
back her head, and says, 'Welcome to the *thee-ah-ter*!'" I
last saw Stella in May 1989 at the Jewish Museum in Phil-
adelphia (and at a reception in Society Hill afterward) for
the opening of an exhibit on Yiddish Theatre celebrating
her father, Jacob Adler. She was using a walker to ease hip
issues. Her cognition and humor were unimpaired. When
Eli Wallach spoke, he called her "a font of truth."

Here are adjectives often ascribed to Stella Adler the
teacher: dynamic, passionate, bold, and flamboyant; poet-
ical, theatrical, and imperious; a tough critic, both harsh
and tender. To me, in near-daily contact with her for two
years and close by for another year including as an actor
directed by her, Stella did not come across as harsh. She was
exacting. She could readily lose patience (like Stanislavsky
lost patience with lazy students) and use uncompromising
words. No actor should miss her reprimand of a young Mark
Ruffalo in the documentary *Stella Adler: Awake and Dream*
from the PBS *American Masters* series; nor should they
neglect to note her forgivingness following the reprimand.

Stella's abiding intention was to teach. It was her
super-objective. To teach, in the manner of Stella, could
manifest as to scold, to castigate, to dismiss, to challenge,
to arouse, to uplift, to encourage. She was thoroughly
pedagogical, and the underpinning of her teaching was
unsentimental compassion. Her regality was a teaching, as
was her flirtatiousness. Her double-takes, chest-baring, and

studio entrances cradling Mookie the Shih Tzu were teachings. Her canny insight, up-to-date-ness, emotional intelligence, and vitality—even her affectations—were teachings. She exuded and modeled the kind of confidence that is not self-centered. Though claiming theatre royalty by virtue of her parentage, she leaned not toward egocentricity. She was a ponderer and reflective, not an ideologue. As my fellow Studio classmate Rick Hendrie reminisced, "She pulled the curtain aside to reveal an alternate universe."

I'd like to note that Robert De Niro told Sheana Ochoa, author of the engaging biography *Stella! Mother of Modern Acting*, that he never cared for Stella's affectedness. Yet he studied script analysis and all the rest with her for three years:

> She made a lot of sense as a teacher. She had a very healthy approach toward acting and technique, although she was a little at odds with the [Actors] Studio and Strasberg and all that, but then she had a great actor, Brando, with her. When I was studying with her, I didn't even know he had studied with her.

There are rumors that Stella was harder on women than on men. It may have been so, but that, too, was not my experience. She once told me I was in possession of masculine and feminine energies in equal proportion (which may have been a more fitting description of Stella's energies than of mine). That mixture, she said, was unusual in a woman and because of it, I would be hard to cast—they couldn't make me an ingenue and they wouldn't put me in comedy. It was half-so with Stella in her acting career. The Group

Theatre did indeed not make her an ingenue but cast her in roles older than her years; however, when it came to Hollywood, they seemed to think she should be funny even if they didn't know what to do with her talent. In Stella's day, ahead of her time, almost post-patriarchal, she challenged young women to enlarge their impact, breaking free of submissive or recessive ways of being and doing, while standing up as substantial beings. She chided women students who brought conventional "little woman" behaviors to the stage that they'd picked up from a male-controlled society and the limitations of a middle-class, family-bound, domesticated upbringing. In short, Stella did not gender-stereotype. Moreover, according to Rose Malague, in contrast with Lee Strasberg and Sandy Meisner, she didn't pursue an agenda to make actresses cry by breaking down their defenses.

She invited students to divest of mediocrity in any shape and to think of themselves as millions of years old, containing the whole history of art and culture, not just *pishers*—insignificant beings—on the street. Her love for students took the form of: I defy you to rise above and beyond the commonplace without hyperbole. As Kate Mulgrew said to me in a 2023 phone conversation, Stella Adler "was an all-or-nothing, Hedda Gabler kind of girl. There was not a cheap note in her music."

A breeze of mysticism lightly encircled Stella's glamorous demeanor. Her politics were progressive. As a secular Jew, she was an early-age activist for human rights. Spiritually, she encouraged us, her students, to feel the spaciousness of being alive, to experience life as limitless, unbounded, universal, miraculous, and ongoing, as it is in the work of Thornton Wilder, whose plays touched her like a lover. (There is a story that Wilder once proposed to her, totally naked, at her doorstep.) After all, when she deigned to give up her evenings to direct former students in a public production, she chose Wilder's *The Happy Journey to Trenton and Camden,* in which I played Ma Kirby. On opening night, when the actress in the role of my fifteen-year-old daughter Caroline arrived at the theatre with the horror of two black eyes administered by a jealous boyfriend, Stella responded from a place of spiritual, as much as professional, dignity. With the gravity of a rabbi, she accepted the appalling situation and gave instruction for whitening the skin around the actress's injured eyes. It's noteworthy that the actress, now known as Karen Rae Kraut, went on to create a lifelong career as a professional storyteller in California. With respect to a quote often (though incorrectly) attributed to Maya Angelou, Karen recently said, "Stella didn't liberate me in terms of an answer, but she did liberate me in terms of a song."

Thornton Wilder wrote, "Saints and poets realize life while living." For Stella, the actor was to be a form of poet, engaged in something earthly and exalted, working not for glamour or money, and giving everything to art. She was a spiritual warrior for the theatre.

PREPARATION FOR THE PATH

For the student, a minimum of two years' training is necessary. For the actor, a lifetime.

Rather than assume everyone agrees on definitions, I want to clarify Stella Adler's understanding of what an actor is; who may best become an actor, and how; and what acting is. In teaching the Character Class (the subject of Chapter IV of this book, "Characterization: Who the Actor Becomes"), Stella devoted several sessions to The Greeks, as she called the classical civilization that created theatre in the fifth century BCE. Her values stemmed, yes, from her parents' Yiddish Theatre; from Stanislavsky and the Moscow Art Theatre; and from Harold Clurman's aspirational philosophy for the Group Theatre; but they also sprang from the artistic values and the dramatic literature of classical Greek theatre. In Stella's dictionary, The Greeks, whose "psychic size" she held in lofty regard, *are* theatre.

So, what is an actor? According to Stella Adler, the actor is the most important member of theatre, who, unlike other artists, works uniquely with his own body, speech, and mind. He is not an entertainer or commercial entity for sale but is a person with a calling.

We know from theatre history that the Greek word *hypokrites* translates into actor or stage player. The word's central idea is someone performing action on a stage. The someone is regarded as an act-or or a play-er. He is not regarded as an emote-er or a feel-er. Furthermore, *hypokrites* is a compound noun made of two words that literally translate as "an interpreter from underneath." Remembering that the actor in ancient Greek theatre wore a mask, the translation makes sense. The actor is an interpreter underneath a mask. The masks of Greek theatre provided generic levels of character identity, thus marking the actor as an interpreter in the guise of someone other than, and decidedly not, himself. The Greek actor's interpretation was communicated through consummate skill in stylized movement and virtuosic delivery of poetic language, based on near-operatic vocal training. Greek actors were supreme performers in a highly esteemed artistic profession.

Well, then, who best may become an actor and how does it happen? In 1957 Stella told the *New York Post,*

"I became an actress because I dreamed my leading men would fall madly in love with me." At a later moment, not in jest, Stella said, "Not everyone, no matter how much training, can become an actor. . . . The essential quality in an actor is the desire to act." A person who desires to act demonstrates some talent for acting, though "real talent can't be discerned easily or quickly." According to Stella, a person wanting to become an actor feels a challenge from within. They see an image and dare themselves to imitate it, whether it's someone in politics or someone on the street. They feel joy in using language and movement for creative expression. "Almost everybody has a little bit of the urge to try to act," Stella said. "But in this life, most people are forced to play only one side of themselves." In the case of the person destined to become an actor, she wrote in *The Technique of Acting*, "All those other selves create a unique unquiet in the actor's soul, and that provokes him to have his talent heard."

As Stella said, while training does not make an actor out of a nonactor, "When the need to act is strong, there must be a place to study, a place to practice, and, finally, a place to perform." A proper place of study is a studio or a school offering an escalating stream of practical techniques forming an overall Technique or System of Acting. Through learning to engage the totality of the techniques, the actor develops a craft. As he learns the craft of acting, his talent comes forward, released by craft. Stella was insistent that talent must be fed if it is ever to first be discerned and then developed. Starting with its embryonic stage, talent may best be nourished by images of seasoned talent. Talent needs a society that reveres the art of acting, a society where a wannabe actor can go to the theatre and behold esteemed actors playing Clytemnestra or King Lear, performing Shakespeare, Moliere, the Greeks, modern European and American giants, and, I daresay, classic Asian plays. In such an environment, the wannabe actor's talent can grow. He will want, even desperately want, to perform as well as the esteemed actors do. Stella noted that talent by its very nature responds to influences, making it flower or making it fade. But in America, how often are audiences seeing Clytemnestra or King Lear? How many mature American actors dare to magnify their range? Where in America is the rich theatrical climate that young actors require for their talent to grow? Stella lamented that the wannabe actor in contemporary America must mostly make do with movies (and, nowadays, video representations on small screens).

Talent responds not only to seeing other talent but also to being seen. Stella said when talent has the opportunity of the platform and the challenge of a good or at least work-able script, it will reveal itself and news of it will spread. She believed there were more American Brandos, Pacinos, and De Niros (and Streeps, I will add) out there in the hinterland who didn't have a place to practice, who didn't have a place to perform, and who didn't have the chance to be seen.

So, if that is the actor, what is acting? Aristotle, philos-opher of Greek theatre, declared that theatre is not narra-tive, is not storytelling, but involves the performance of an overall action of a certain magnitude, that is, story-en-acting. Theatre is an overall action dramatized with the accompaniment of embellished language. As Stella often iterated, acting is not a matter of being "real" or "natural" or "playing to the minimal," as if the actor's job is to depict so-called real life. Acting is neither talking and gesturing nor yelling and feeling. As detailed in Chapter III of this book ("Action: What the Actor Does"), acting is *doing* a simple or complex psycho-physical action that has a goal and is justified by the character's motivation. The action is won or lost, there is a transition, and a new sequence (often called a beat) begins. I think it's better to use Adler's term "sequence" rather than the more often heard "beat" to demarcate a section of text in which an action is played. I worked with a director who instructed student actors to write an action on every line of text. I don't know if the director, preposterously, meant a *different* action on every line; but if an actor tried to play a different action on every line, they would put themselves into fragmented chaos. An action is pursued and sustained until it is won or lost. An action, beyond a moment in time, may well extend over several pages of text.

Stella's picture of the graduate leaving her Studio is the picture of an actor with craft in hand commencing a life-long practice toward revealing his own humanity. Stella said, "You can't be an actor unless you're an adult."

THE PATH

There are actors who transform and there are actors who don't.

Let's now look toward the path leading to the development of the Artist–Human Being. Let's begin with the baseline actor, that is, the actor who has the talent and craft to build a performance but does not seek to embrace the creative work of an artist. The baseline actor plays some version of himself, similarly from role to role. With each new role, the name of the character and his lines change, and so does the costume the actor wears and maybe his hair's style or color. But the way in which the actor moves, talks, and behaves doesn't change substantially, role to role. This is a self-referential kind of acting dependent upon the actor emphasizing similarities between himself and the character and ignoring or downplaying the differences. He fits the character to himself, making use of his own life experiences to play the role. In time, he becomes dependent upon what he did in the last role to play the next role. His acting may well be believable. It may be considered good acting, but it is not the art of acting.

Stella Adler didn't say doing a self-portrait unequivocally results in bad acting. She did say if an actor plays some version of himself, duping the audience into believing that the characterization he's bringing to the stage or screen is the role as it was written, that is a bad actor. A good actor, true to the intention of the profession (that is, to "interpret from under the mask") doesn't use himself as the character. In the entire history of acting, as Adler pointed out, no notable actor played himself. Sarah Siddons never played Mrs. Siddons and Henry Irving never played Mr. Irving. The actors that history remembers played characters.

I first saw Mark Ruffalo in the 2000 film *You Can Count on Me*. I didn't know his name or anything about him, but as I was watching and asking myself, "Who is this actor?", I was also thinking, "I bet he studied with Stella Adler." My inkling was in response to the inner life coming through his performance. You could see him thinking, and he seemed to be thinking not as the actor but as the ne'er-do-well brother Terry, as if weighing things from the character's point of view. You couldn't be certain what either the character Terry, or the un-programmatic Mark Ruffalo, was going to do next. Sure enough, back home, checking the internet, I confirmed Mark Ruffalo had studied with Stella Adler.

Stella said, "Don't make your standard or scale: 'I am *me* and I like *me* and I'm going to show *me*!'—hoping they'll buy you the way they buy the cloud or the rain they need for the shot." She warned against "showing yourself on stage (or screen) because you think you're special: you're not special." The individual actor is a unique combination of qualities, but not special. She urged against a self-portrait kind of acting:

> Always keep yourself out of it. Say to yourself, "I, myself, don't count. The world counts. If I'm beautiful, it's not my beauty that's important in my actions. It's not the suffering side of me that's important, but what I do." . . . In life, as on the stage, it's not who I am but what I do that's the measure of my worth and the secret of my success. All the rest is showiness, arrogance, and conceit.

Instead of "I'm going to show *me*," Stella offered a different standard: "Every actor is suited to play more than what they look like."

The major causes of self-portrait acting are insubstantial imagination and inadequate script analysis. It's the actor's responsibility to play in the imagined circumstances of the script. Stella held that there is not any circumstance in the life of any actor that directly corresponds to the circumstances of a character's life—none! If I use my own life circumstances to play the play, what have I created? How have I invoked, or have I rejected, my imagination? How have I respected, or have I manipulated, the script? If I use my own circumstances to play the play, I deny myself access to the realm of art. Emotion memory is no substitute for imagination. Using clues from my own life doesn't equal creating the character's life. Emotion memory and personal cues can be enormously helpful in warming up to, even figuring out, what the character may be going through, and there's the end to them. Using imagination, I create the given circumstances, based on script analysis, to get grounded in the life of the play and get out of my own life. Stella asserted, "Using the circumstances of the script leads to great acting. Being in one's own circumstances is what kills acting in America."

Here's the Adler truth of it all: "When a man puts on a costume, he also gives up something of himself, his personal self, for something bigger. The costume obliterates the petty self." Still, Stella worried, "We live in times when men aren't willing to deny the self."

This thing called self is fundamentally a super-obstacle for whoever aspires to the art of acting. Here's how Marlon Brando described the dilemma in his autobiography, *Brando: Songs My Mother Taught Me*, referring to fellow actors:

> [Actors] work so hard at becoming successful that when they reach the top, they become cautious and try to do the same thing over and over again, because they're frightened of playing a part in which they may fall on their faces. [Robert] Duvall takes chances and has fallen on his face, but far more times than not he has established a characterization that is not Duvall. He's a wonderful actor.

> The same can be said of Al Pacino. When I met him
> on *The Godfather* he was quite troubled. Since then,
> he's . . . shown that he is willing to take a chance
> and not be afraid where he's going to land.

Brando added that the screen stars of the 1940s who preceded him never changed their look, "like breakfast loops." To Brando there was something ludicrous—"their gestures become absurd"—in acting the same way in every role. Actors, he said, mustn't stop "taking dares."

A big impediment to "taking dares" is the box office. People pay to see an actor repeatedly play himself—though actually, what he's more likely doing is repeatedly playing a type. As Tom Oppenheim wrote, "The tendency in America to associate success with money causes actors to figure out their type and stick to it." Tom also placed blame for self-referential acting on the industry: "The fast pace at which they work in film causes producers, directors, and casting agents to look not for an actor who can *play* the character, but for the character himself . . . and encourages casting agents . . . [to] find someone who does not have to *act*. Many a teacher and director repeat the same battle cry: 'Just be yourself.'"

Some film actors are so striking or strikingly beautiful in and of themselves, they are akin to public sculptures—sculptures that move. Idolized for their model bodies and faces, they don't deviate from their familiar image from role to role. The rewards for appearing and reappearing as a fixed form of moving visual art are money and celebrity. And now audiences, at home with screens, can pretend intimacy with a celebrity actor—a famously attractive person in our living rooms who appears accessible, like a best friend, on talk shows. Responsibility for this false familiarity may also lie with the publicity division of the entertainment industry.

The actor playing himself, or repeating a type, hands over control of his career to producers and the public. He allows himself to some extent to be owned by them. That is the *ethical* reason why Stella Adler called the *me*-actor a bad actor.

Here's my explanation for how playing oneself is artistically problematic. If I'm a skillful and talented portrait painter, my painting of Jacqueline Kennedy isn't going to look like my painting of Eleanor Roosevelt, and it certainly isn't going to look like me. The public may recognize my style as the painter of both Mrs. Kennedy and Mrs. Roosevelt, and that, indeed, is a fine outcome—an artist with a recognizable style. The situation ought to be no different with acting. If I'm playing Amanda in *Glass Menagerie*, I would not have her talking, walking, looking, or behaving like Mary Tyrone of *Long Day's Journey*. And I would not have Amanda or Mary Tyrone walking, talking, behaving, or thinking like me. My actorly mark, a kind of signature, will distinguish my Amanda from another actor's Amanda. In short, an actor painting the same portrait, time and again, may deliver credibly good acting. But as their acting is grounded more in duplication than in imagination, it doesn't an art form make. That is the *artistic* reason why Stella Adler called the *me*-actor a bad actor.

Stella said, "Motion pictures have given the average person the sense they can act. Mostly, the average person can do only a part of acting, not the whole of it." Average persons can walk and talk and learn lines and some can say the lines convincingly. That's why average persons sense they can act. Average persons are bewitched by the mistaken idea that talent in performance is playing oneself.

In his masterful book *The Method: How the Twentieth Century Learned to Act,* Isaac Butler places our current society in a Time of Performance: "Due in no small part to social media, we are more conscious than ever that we are performing for an audience of other people. We are also aware that we are the audience for everyone else's performances, and we rate them, not with applause, but with hearts and thumbs-up. . . . It is unsettling to always be at least slightly aware that nothing is real, least of all ourselves."

Butler is aptly describing a reality rarely cognized, more rarely experienced, and most rarely admitted: that we (unenlightened) human beings fabricate a self to live our life. That is not in the least to say that we don't exist. It is to say that we don't exist in the way we assume we do. We do indeed fashion a self, though I daresay the fashioning is not a new or modern phenomenon. The fabrication of a self has always been the (unenlightened) mode of human beings. The difference between prior times and now is that today, as Butler points out, nearly everyone's fabrication has to some extent gone public. Our public self-presentation answers an American appetite for self-promotion. Almost everybody—not just politicians, pundits, preachers, podcast hosts, and talking journalists—is into "let me show you *me*." Who doesn't have a story for the radio hour? Citizens show up at political rallies arrayed in costume and carrying signs as props, ready to be interviewed, photographed, or videoed. There's a pervasive giddiness about *me* being seen, being heard, being noticed, and not being ignored. As Harold Clurman would say, "The world has a jag on."

I reluctantly lay our weird societal situation, our Time of Performance, at the feet of professional actors who've made acting look like it's nothing but playing yourself. Self-portrait actors, urged on by producers and directors and cheered on by teachers of acting, have precipitated the Time of Performance. Altogether they have disregarded the original idea, the Greek ideal, that the mask is vital to the *art* of acting. The Greeks found honor in representing a character that is not oneself. Denying the origins of theatre, the *me*-actor betrays the profession. That is the *spiritual* reason why Stella Adler called him a bad actor.

For the sake of goodwill, I'd like to replace the word "bad" with "underdeveloped" or "lightly developed." The actor who repeats a type or a version of himself is entrapped. He may be fearful of the public or compromised by producers. He deserves our condolence, our sympathy and sadness, for confining himself to the base level of an actor's development.

DEVELOPMENT OF THE ACTOR-ARTIST

Acting is human behavior assembled into a character, and then reassembled into another character, in new and interesting ways!

The Greek word *hypokrites* (once again, meaning a stage actor) ultimately came into English as "hypocrite"—that is, a person who puts on a false appearance as if their own. Regardless of the fact that hypocrite has a negative meaning in English, it's a fitting description of the next level of an actor's development: Actor-Artist, the actor who creates an identity different from his own.

One of Stella Adler's earliest memories was watching

her father in the dressing room, putting on his makeup: "There was a special quality in this choosing of his colors, and placing them, like a painter, one next to the other, an almost religious sense of something being created. I watched this creation. I watched a man change into another man." That "almost religious sense" is the epitome of this level of development: to change into another person. The Greeks put on masks, platform shoes, and non-streetwear costumes, and with non-pedestrian movement and vocal aerobics, they altered themselves. In the modern theatre, in the style of realism, alteration is likewise needed to qualify for the *art* of acting.

In Stevan Riley's 2015 documentary *Listen to Me Marlon,* Marlon Brando described acting as putting yourself in a different state of mind that goes into the part. Characterization, he said, is a process of "putting on a mask, building a life, and then suddenly something gets a hold of you . . . and you 'hold the mirror up to nature.'" Regarding his role in *A Streetcar Named Desire*, he wrote, "Absolutely nothing about me [was] like Stanley Kowalski."

It's rather more evident with classical theatre to see how the character is not oneself. The differences between then and now in time and place alone, not to mention social stratification, are stark. Though it may by now be a well-known anecdote, one of the funniest things that ever came from the mind of Stella Adler was when an aspiring actor said he could play the role of Hamlet because Hamlet was just like him. Stella looked at the young man, up and down. She paused, and then she roared, "Hamlet owns Denmark!"

In the style of realism, it takes some investigation to see how the character is not oneself. In 2004 I performed the role of Stella Adler in an unpublished play called *The Group* by Ronald Rand, based on memories of the Group Theatre, at the Players Club in New York. When you play a real person, whose characteristics are observable, you perceive how much you as an actor can and should change yourself to take on, at the very least, intimations of the voice and movement of that not-me real person. This precise consideration—how is the character different from me?—is the basis for the Actor-Artist operating in the style of realism.

When I was a student taking Character Class at the Adler Studio, Stella instructed us to gather on stage, walk every which way, and make sincere eye contact with every other student. I walked into the middle of the group and a truly tall, dark, and handsome man walked toward me. It was the first day of class and I hadn't yet noticed him. We looked into each other's eyes and, *blam*, fell in love. He was Cuban-born, a working actor in Spanish-language movies and television, who had come to the Adler Studio with the aspiration to work in English-speaking film. Partway into the semester, after our class had studied the Greeks and practiced the behavior of the Aristocracy, followed by the Clergy, Stella turned us toward the Peasantry. Carlos Badias—for that was his name—was unwilling to enact the behavior of a Brueghel-like peasant or interact with people playing peasants. The culture of medieval peasantry for Carlos, whose ancestors were Barcelonian nobility, was a descent too far.

Transformation requires some measure of the quality of empathy, and empathy is not automatically accessible. Likewise, transformation, a vastly creative undertaking, is not always workable. Not all actors rise to their potential.

Stella let Carlos sit out the Peasantry class. But when he

and I, in Scene Study class, were performing the bedroom episode from Jean Cocteau's *The Eagle with Two Heads*, in which he was playing Stanislas (a poet turned anarchist and potential suicidal assassin), Stella came onstage after the scene, reached up to take Carlos's broad shoulders in her hands, and shook him like a dusty throw rug. It wasn't Stella's custom to manhandle students. But in the case of Carlos, she grabbed hold, apparently wanting utterly to unsettle his conceptions of himself; and beyond his shoulders she shook his attachment to an aristocratic demeanor. Our classmate Dan Merchant, recalling the incident years later, said it signified how "Stella could reach into a place of fire inside and get you to ignite it." The fire waiting to be ignited is the empathy needed for transformation.

What is a character? We know by now that a character is not the actor. A character is an imaginary being (even if based on a real person) that comes alive by means of the actor's pursuit of the overall aim of the character, known as the super-objective. The fact is that character creation can and does happen; an actor can manifest in detail the outside of a character and devise for him a complex inner life. How it happens is due to technique and a kind of magic, or better, a mystery. Magic turns an actor into an Actor-Artist.

Stella said, "A truly creative performance, conceived and executed by the actor, is a complex process. It is impossible to discern which part stems from the conscious and which from the subconscious—they cannot be separated. Such a creative expression cannot be analyzed, either by the creator or by Freud and his followers."

Using script analysis and not psychoanalysis, the actor figures out how the character responds to the social code depicted in the play. The character always exists in a place even if the setting is "nowhere." The place is always imaginary, even if the setting is an actual address on Flatbush Avenue. Through careful reading and analysis, the actor comes to know the nature of the place. The place includes the other character(s). The place includes the values held by the community: its way of life in raising children, its treatment of a minority group, its religious beliefs, its modes of entertainment, etc. The place tells the character what action to take about where he is and who he is with. Stella said, "When you don't understand the place, you have to act," by which she meant fake-act. "The place" is another name for the "given circumstances." Stella said, "The most important thing in opening the play is to know the circumstances." She advised, "Know the given circumstances like your blood."

Whether devised theatre, nontraditional theatre, physical theatre, or scripted theatre, there is always a Character in a Place. Whether the character is Hamlet or Fat Ham, Antigone or Alice in Wonderland, Shakuntala or Mother Courage, Troy Maxton, Estragon, or Joan of Arc, or a tree or a dog or milk, or clouds or rain or energy, the actor represents someone, or something, who exists someplace, even if the place is "nowhere," at some time, even if the time is "forever," with an action to fulfill, even if the action is static. Those are the given circumstances: who I am, where I am, when I am there, who I am with, and what do I need to do about it. That's the actor's ground that Stella stood for.

In addition to script analysis, the other ingredient in creating a character is imagination. Coming from the realm of the intangible, imagination has the power to defictionalize fiction. Imagination enables the actor to believe in the reality of an unreal situation. If I'm playing Gertrude, Queen of Denmark, I walk and talk as I imagine Gertrude would, based on all I've gleaned about Gertrude's given circumstances in the play called *Hamlet*. Imagination gives the actor histrionic truth, letting him drop his personal habits and respond physically in new ways.

Marlon Brando was a resoundingly imaginative actor attentive to the inner as well as outer elements of a role. He said, "You have to know your character, their mind, put yourself in their place, and figure out a way to do it that's not been done before." Harold Clurman recognized in Brando an enormous curiosity about people that transferred to his interest in characterization. By his own admission, Brando preserved his sanity in the unreasonable world of Hollywood by creating a gallery of characters. Getting out of his own life (and leaving behind the other characters he'd previously played), Brando was able to avoid succumbing to mental confusion while on the set. Every portrait he created, some legendarily memorable, was different, and always there was his signature.

Marlon Brando's description of how he built the role of Don Corleone in *The Godfather* is in sync with Stella Adler's steps for creating a character. It's well-known how Brando constructed a mask for the audition, using makeup and shoe-polish and stuffing Kleenex in his cheeks. As for finding the personality of the Godfather, here's what he wrote in his autobiography:

> Rather than portraying him as a big shot, I thought it would be more effective to play him as a modest, quiet man, the way he was in the book. Don Corleone was part of the wave of immigrants who came to this country and had to swim upstream to survive

as best they could. As a young man, he probably hadn't intended to become a criminal, and when he did, he hoped it would be transitional. . . .

I thought it would be interesting to play a gang-ster . . . who wasn't like those bad guys Edward G. Robinson played, but who was a . . . man to be respected. Also, because he had so much power and unquestioned authority, I thought it would be an interesting contrast to play him as a gentle man, unlike Al Capone, who beat up people with baseball bats. I had a great deal of respect for Don Corleone; I saw him as a man of substance, tradition, dignity, refinement, a man of unerring instinct who just happened to live in a violent world and who had to protect himself and his family in this environment. I saw him as a decent person regardless of what he had to do, as a man who believed in family values and was shaped by events just like the rest of us. . . . Don Corleone fought back, and this was the story of *The Godfather*. He would not surrender to the men who demanded a piece of everyone's action. He was forced to protect his family, and in the pro-cess, he gravitated into crime.

Characterization is the creative aspect of acting. It's a matter of script analysis plus imagination unleashing talent. It's the excitement of transformation, the truth of imper-manence of oneself, and the joy of acting!

In the year 2006, Clifford Odets's Bronx-family drama, *Awake and Sing!*, enjoyed a revival on Broadway. Of course, Stella Adler had premiered the matriarchal role of Bessie Berger in the original Group Theatre production in 1935. In the revival, Mark Ruffalo was playing the tricky role of Moe Axelrod. According to the *New York Times* review, "nobody slings [Odets's snazzy language] with more panache than Mark Ruffalo." A group of five, all former Adler Studio students, reunited in New York to see *Awake and Sing!* from front-row seats in honor of Stella and to appreciate the work of her former student. After the performance, we five waited for Ruffalo outside the stage door where fans had gathered. We were hanging near the back, as he came out, greeted people, signed autographs, and started to move on. I stepped forward and, eye to eye with Mark Ruffalo, I congratulated him on the performance. And then I said, "I studied with Stella." Upon hearing Stella's name and seeing this person in front of him as a fellow-Stella-traveler, his countenance filled with joy, utter unalloyed joy. He took my face in his hands, and he kissed me.

The live character is the true center of theatre art. Regarding the subject of this book's Chapter II, "The Resources of the Actor," Stella encouraged her students to make great use of the life of the world and the life of materials to make a good mask, and to lean heavily on costume as the best, sometimes the only, avenue to creating an inner self for the character. With a good mask and the right costume, the actor can relax; and with relaxation he can travel to the next stage on the path of acting: the interpretation of ideas.

DEVELOPMENT OF THE ACTOR-CITIZEN

You have to accept responsibility for civilization.

Stella envisioned the actor as "a bearer of poetry and truth." The truths the actor bears have to do with the behavior of human beings in social (sometimes social-polit-ical) situations that are universal, occurring and reoccurring all over the world. Actors get to these truths, or "big ideas" as she called them, by means of script analysis (the subject of Chapter V of this book, "Text: What the Actor Knows"). A big idea has scope and carries moral force. In classical the-atre, the big ideas may be found in the words. In the style of realism, the big ideas are often found beneath the words. In film, where language is not particularly important, the actor may need visuals from the director to help convey the big ideas.

Stella Adler gave us tools for analyzing scripts unlike and well beyond anyone else in American actor training. (See her two books on play analysis, edited by Barry Paris: *Stella Adler on Ibsen, Strindberg and Chekhov* and *Stella Adler on America's Master Playwrights.*) According to the research of Isaac Butler, both Bobby Lewis and Uta Hagen used script analysis in teaching scene study; Lee Strasberg and Sandy Meisner did not promote the practice. "Script analysis," Stella said, "serves as the actor's armor against self-indulgence!"

Stella's attraction to great plays distinguishes her approach to script analysis, as does her thoroughness and steadfast "digging down" into the lines of a scene for something very real—a trace of human truth—to pop up. Her father, Jacob Adler, modeled the appreciation of dramatic literature; he transformed the Yiddish Theatre in New York from entirely lightweight and melodramatic to a roster including Shake-speare and Schiller and modern works from Ibsen to Victor Hugo to Shaw. Stella went further, expecting actors to develop their creative intelligence by becoming knowledge-able in all the arts. Her advice was, "Turn off the television and listen to music. Read good books, read a lot of poetry, join societies where you can read aloud to each other."

Script analysis is foundational. It gives the actor intellectual independence. Neither subservient nor in thrall to the director, he's not beholden simply to fulfill the director's vision of the play. By studying and analyzing the given circumstances of the script, the actor discovers the character's super-objective as well as the relationships between characters. The relationships point to the big ideas. Knowing the big ideas allows the actor to become personally involved with the playwright's vision. He figures out where the playwright stands and where his character stands in relation to the play's social situation. (Some actors—all actors, in a Brechtian theatre— may also want to figure out where they stand or would like to stand or are challenged to stand in relation to the playwright, ideologically.) Skillful script analysis makes the actor a trustworthy script *interpreter*. One of my favorite Adler recommendations is to change the name of the profession from acting to script interpretation, so people may comprehend that actors are not idiots.

The actor isn't a parrot, just speaking words he doesn't understand. He learns to sense the power and quality of ideas expressed by important playwrights who are trying to get at how things really are in the body politic, in domestic relations, and in the human condition. Playwrights may reveal, for example, the brutality of class systems, corruption of religious institutions, hypocrisies of family life, and the individual's capacity for self-delusion. The actor speaks (directly or indirectly) to the audience, as an interpreter of the vision of someone (the playwright) whose ideas matter. As Stella suggested, the actor who interprets is of interest to the audience. Interpretation warms up the audience and they draw closer. In this way, as a person of interest, the actor impresses the ideas of the play upon the audience that they may better understand their lives.

When the actor takes responsibility for physicalizing the theme (also called the spine) of the play, he ascends to the level of Actor-Citizen, where acting becomes, in part, a public service vocation. As Stella declared, if the actor can't convey a deep understanding of the play to the audience, then acting is self-indulgence without a social purpose.

What does the actor need to convey big ideas? "Size," Stella said, "is the name of the game. . . . Size must be awakened in the actor so he can understand big ideas." Stella insisted that, first, to awaken size, the actor forsakes his identification with the middle class. She characterized middle-class values as the product of institutional thinking based on conformity meant to conceal the truth. The goal of the Actor-Citizen is to participate in revealing, not concealing, things that are true.

To awaken size, the actor expands and enhances his familiarity with the history of theatre, art, and culture. He goes to concerts and museums, and he reads and studies. His attentiveness to culture deepens his sense of responsibility toward examining the social situation inherent in plays, and it gives him confidence in his capability to ponder, for example, the role and treatment of women in the society of a play.

The work of major playwrights can't be expressed properly except by actors interested in big ideas. The Citizen-Actor examines how Arthur Miller, for example, wants to say something not only about Willy Loman, the salesman, but about an American way of life based on buying and selling and the deadly effects of commodification on human beings. The Citizen-Actor doesn't limit the mind of Miss Alma of Tennessee Williams' *Summer and Smoke* to that of a spinster daughter of a Christian minister; rather, she perceives an angel struggling with sexual corporeality in the face of medical science. As Stella said, the size of the character must exist within the actor. He can't pretend it or borrow it. In other words, to play Hamlet, he needs to exercise intellect. To play Antigone or Beneatha Youngers, she needs social consciousness. Cultivating the size of the Actor-Citizen, the actor stretches beyond habitual or limited concepts, opening to new and big ideas. That is why Stella taught The Greeks, for the student to expand in size.

The Actor-Citizen reaches for the historic size of the profession. The Greek theatre was a theatrical enterprise incorporating sacred, secular, civic, artistic, and natural realms into a unified artwork concerned with moral consequences. Greek playwrights took stories from ancient Greek epics, and their dramatizations of the stories reflected contemporary social-political concerns, as we may nowadays witness overtly in a Tony Kushner or a Lorraine Hansberry play. The Greek theatre operated in part as a forum to air conflicting points of view. In this sense, the Greek theatre, seating more than ten thousand people side by side on benches made of stone in a massive outdoor semicircle, served as a place of healing for the body politic.

In a profession for men only, the Greek actor was able to rise from any walk of life (except slave) and was exempted from military service because of performing an esteemed civic function—interpretation of the concerns of the day. His profession helped people to understand the ethical, secular, and spiritual significance of their lives and society. He was a kind of celebrant—sometimes civil, sometimes medicinal, sometimes priestly. Some Greek actors, in the months of the year when plays weren't being performed, served as government emissaries, further expanding the territory and impact of the Actor-Citizen.

Marlon Brando was a devoted script interpreter. (See Scott Balcerzak's interesting book *Beyond Method: Stella Adler and the Male Actor*, particularly his discerning chapter on Brando's extraordinary skill in characterization.) Brando used the given circumstances to express the social situation of the play and the big ideas of the playwright. Take the example of his behavior as Stanley Kowalski in Tennessee Williams's *A Streetcar Named Desire* at the gloomy birthday dinner party of his sister-in-law Blanche DuBois. After being chastised for crude table manners by his wife Stella, Stanley violently sweeps his dishes from the kitchen table like an ape in confusion (as Blanche sees him) or like a king countering a threat upon his castle (as Stanley sees himself). Stanley's physical action culminates in the line "Now, that's how I'm gonna clear the table." His destruction of the table setting highlights a theme of the play: rising American authoritarianism (exemplified by Stanley) is ruthlessly displacing traditional gentility, already in deterioration (per Blanche's circumstances). After all, Tennessee Williams wrote Stanley Kowalski as an American war veteran, mobile in the business world, and captain of the bowling team!

To speak as the Actor-Citizen was one of Brando's manifold gifts. Brando, through his physical choices as Stanley—how he moved the muscular parts of his body, how he chewed gum and grinned, how he pretended he didn't mind that he didn't know what he was talking about, how he destroyed things when he felt undermined, how he cried and bellowed for his wife Stella—made Stanley provocative, magnetic, sexually compelling, and alluringly vulnerable. With Brando's interpretation, we witness the appeal of brutality. His Stanley has the primordial attractiveness of a virile man on the make who fights to win and will rape you if you're a "noisy" (culturally superior) woman opposing him. Here's how Stella Adler understood Stanley: "He lacks [Blanche's] spiritual strength. Out of . . . enraged frustration, he attacks what he cannot attain."

If Jessica Tandy on stage in 1947 had been able to render Blanche DuBois more endearing, more sympathetic, more emotionally intelligent than flighty, and as spiritually persevering as Williams wrote her, audiences would not have cheered Stanley's rape of Blanche, as it is said they vocally did in the theatre of 1947. If there had been more balance in the struggle between Stanley and Blanche, then the mid-century audience may have apprehended Tennessee Williams's big idea: that the callous, upwardly mobile energy of the uncultivated and minimally educated American male is exciting; and that as this American male rises to dominance—without artistic or intellectual culture, without a seat in historic tradition, but with a sense of ownership and prerogative—he veers toward fascism. In the poker night scene, Williams allowed Stanley's neighborhood compatriots to roughhouse him but not to ostracize him for his insatiable need to win. At the end of *Streetcar*, the locals choose to stick with Stanley, rationalizing his crimes and failing Blanche in her suffering. Brando's performance revealed the playwright's big ideas. In creating Stanley, Brando made the tough guy, with his anger and his cruelty, magnetic and sexually appealing. Through Stanley, Brando, in respect of Williams, revealed how crowd-captivating, how beguiling, how self-serving the despot (today known as the strong man) may be.

Then there is evermore the issue of having great, or even good, playwrighting for the actor to interpret. Years before our theatre suffered the current scarcity of new playwrights, Stella Adler noted, "We live in a time and country where men aren't comfortable with language." Where are the scripts of today, vibrating with unconventional, imaginative, insightful, stage-worthy language? Clifford Odets's language shot bullets. Tennessee Williams's language implored us not to hang back with the apes. In Arthur Miller's language, the woods are burning. Eugene O'Neill wrote in the language of us fog people. Lorraine Hansberry spoke of a time when freedom used to be life but now it's money. David Mamet cautioned, Don't open your mouth until you know the shot. August Wilson wrote as one born to a time of fire. David Rabe knew that we are our own biggest distractions. Sam Shepard asked, Where are the men? I'm asking, Where are the playwrights? In reference to playwrighting, Tina Howe said, "All of it is true. None of it happened." That, precisely, is the nature of playwrighting: using non-everyday language to speak the reality of what is, though it never happened. Actors take what never happened and make it happen.

And still, an actor of size, a Citizen-Actor, can save a play. He can enlarge what a writer is minimally or barely saying. In 2022 I was part of a Zoom series hosted by the Adler Studio for the education of acting teachers in training. Benicio del Toro, as a visiting guest presenter, was explaining how the search for big ideas, which he learned from studying with Stella Adler, motivates his work. Through her, he became "interested in the human condition," which led him to approach characterization with sincerity and compassion. His actorly aim, he said, is to tell someone else's story, using research and imagination "to get into their shoes," and then to uplift the character to represent a whole class of humanity. One of the students asked what happens if the script he's working on doesn't have any big ideas. "Then I put them in," he answered.

Here is the point of the Actor-Citizen: he's arrived at an interpretation of an idea worth sharing. If he's lucky, his part is conceived in stage-worthy language. Otherwise, he has size enough, and is awake enough, to convey a big idea physically. Enrichment is the result, for everybody. The Actor-Citizen, like a secular celebrant, elevates the moral consciousness of the audience and, by extension, the civic integrity of the society at large.

DEVELOPMENT OF THE ARTIST–HUMAN BEING

The most important thing the actor has to work on is his mind.

The ultimate level of the actor's path, the development of the Artist–Human Being, is about training the inner person. The Greeks must have revealed and cultivated spiritual qualities within themselves, or they could not have created the art of acting. Theatre history depicts the Greek actor as "beside himself" as he "releases from the fetters of personality." Before the Greeks invented theatre, they performed at religious festivals as dancers and chorus members in styles both lyrical and narrative. With the emergence of the playwright, the festival performances evolved from storytelling to story-enacting and so theatre was born.

With the birth of theatre, the Greeks aspired to transcendence. Ideally, the Greek actor, through the art of acting, set himself aside. He freed his mind of identification with himself. He transcended self, dropping the persona that burdened his daily life. He became one with the role, and if a member of the Chorus, he became one with all.

The quality of transcendence, when realized by Greek actors, led to wide-ranging communion with each other and with the whole clan. A Greek actor could experience a (perhaps intermittent) state of non-separation or non-othering with his fellow actors and with the audience (the clan). This "communion" among Greek actors could provide a sense of spiritual consanguinity—among themselves and by extension between them and the theatregoers. In our day, there is ensemble acting as a means of intimacy among players. Reportedly, ensemble playing was achieved by the Moscow Art Theatre in the time of Stanislavsky to a degree never before seen. Stella Adler's attendance at the MAT in the Soviet Union with Clurman and Strasberg in 1934, as well as her Group Theatre experience, convinced her that actors need an interdependent troupe on stage and an audience providing "noise and warmth" out front.

I recently visited the ancient Greek theatre at Epidaurus, with flawless acoustics and seating for seventeen thousand patrons. Thanks to historic restorations, it is still in use. A short walk from the theatre, one comes upon massive ruins of a sixth-century-BCE sanctuary that was dedicated to the god Asklepios, renowned for the gift of healing. The Greeks considered Epidaurus the birthplace of the art of medicine, and the Asklepios sanctuary was a destination for pilgrims seeking health and well-being. The theatre, built to perfection into the slope of a mount, was added to the sanctuary environs in the fourth century BCE in part for the psychological support and comfort of wayfarers seeking health from Asklepios. The Golden Age of Greece conceived both the art of medicine and the art of theatre as forms of healing.

Learning from the Greeks, and Stella Adler would agree, we may say that the actor's ideal is to experience a profoundly selfless encounter with the condition of being human, alive on stage. When the curtain is rising, an alternate state of mind may take over—a state of heightened, or present-moment, awareness. Stella pushed students to do the homework properly so they could let consciousness do its job. She told students to learn the Technique so they could "throw out the *lousy* Technique!" As relaxation takes hold and the discursive mind shuts up, the actor can enter the now. He may even stay in the now, with presence, for the duration of a scene, not necessarily remembering much of anything afterward. That's the optimal outcome of learning the Technique—a selfless encounter shared interconnectedly with fellow actors in the presence of the clan. It's the accomplishment of the Artist–Human Being; and the Artist–Human Being, I believe, is, deep down, what the actor wants to become.

Stella's teaching was subtlety imbued with a healthy, even practical, mysticism. The way she saw it, we have inherited the collective knowledge and wisdom of our ancestors. The actor, through the energy of imagination (which he has cultivated), can retrieve this inherited knowledge and wisdom, just as if he had lived in other times and places. He can imaginatively create an alternate reality (the world of the play) and live there as if it is real. In addition, Stella said, "The actor, throughout history, has always had a deep and cosmic understanding." This cosmic in-tune-ness lets the actor-artist instinctively understand human nature and human behavior. In my estimation, while realms of consciousness are available to us all, it's the artist (and the bodhisattva or the saint) who can intuitively embrace them.

Stella shared Harold Clurman's view that the quality most lacking in American civilization is spirituality, though she often called it "universality." Clurman, who held Stella central in his life for nearly twenty years and then persuaded her to marry him and stay married to him for another seventeen years, described her as "spiritually vibrant: as if forever awaiting redemption of a faith both substantially realistic and emotionally exalted." The faith Clurman mentions sounds like Stella's idea of acting: realistic (in the sense of true to nature) and exalted. I think she longed not necessarily for redemption but for the clear light of present-moment awareness. She believed in the power of acting to get the actor out of his head and into the now.

Stella's contact with Stanislavsky in the 1930s likely affirmed the spiritual vibrancy that Clurman recognized in her when he and she became acquainted in the 1920s. By the time I studied with her in the 1970s, her view of how to live seemed free of mundanity. She recognized aliveness everywhere, and, in general, wasn't reductive of people, places, things, and ideas. Her instruction was, "Respect everything. If you insist on being casual all day long, you will finally become un-caring." We were requested to discipline ourselves not through psychotherapy ("It doesn't belong in the theatre") but through self-examination and self-reflection.

Back in the 1970s, eight Adler Studio graduates formed, and sustained for two years, what we called the Adler

Group. Seven of us remain. The eighth was Ron Burrus, who taught Adler's Technique in New York and Los Angeles until his death in 2023. Six of us were directed by Stella in Thornton Wilder's *Happy Journey*. Five of the six were the core of the Group. (Ron was the *Happy Journey* sixth.) We five—now residing from LA to Providence—have reunited from time to time in the twenty-first century. All of us, sometime after leaving Stella, independently cultivated a Buddhist-inspired contemplative practice, with particular emphasis on meditation, and have been practitioners ever since. We recently discovered that Ron Burrus had also practiced meditation, as taught by Krishnamurti. I'm tempted to trace our Buddhist dispositions to Stella, even to working together on the Thornton Wilder play under her direction, but I won't. What I will say, is that an awareness of something far more compelling than the *me*-show dawned in each of us during our end-days at the Studio.

I'd like to suggest that Stella Adler naturally, and probably unconsciously, held a dharmic view. She spoke like a Buddhist—an accidental Buddhist. I think my sense of Stella's inadvertent inclination toward the Buddha dharma is borne out by Isaac Butler's representation that "modern acting—in Stella Adler's formulation—evolved to show the fundamental mysteriousness, the inconclusiveness, the *insolvability* of human beings and their problems in the twentieth century." While the Buddha dharma wouldn't say modern life is insolvable, full stop, it would say that life, anytime, anyplace, is insolvable in the ways human beings customarily go about trying to solve it. The Buddha dharma would say that it's our confusion that leads to suffering. Our suffering, whether dramatic or comedic or both, and our questions about how to live, as well as the possibility of wisdom and compassion, is the stuff of great plays.

In the years since Stella's death, theatre historians have expanded our information about Stanislavsky and spirituality: in particular, that he was a student of the philosophy of yoga and its limbs—including concentration, the movement of prana by way of breathing exercise, and asanas—as preludes to the practice of meditation. I don't know if Stella was aware of the yogic Stanislavsky. But I'm disposed to think that, if she were alive today, she would recommend contemplative practices for her students' inner exploration—namely, mindfulness/awareness, also known as tranquility/insight practice. She might hire a teacher to offer meditation classes at the Studio (just as her Studio offered voice and body classes). As is presented in this book's Chapter I, "The Development of the Actor," Stella encouraged students to get their bodies and voices fixed up to make themselves "material" for acting; nowadays, she'd encourage students to get their mental states fixed up.

If Stella were alive today, she'd be aware of the research in the field of neuroscience documenting effects of mindfulness/awareness practices. She'd recommend meditation not simply for relaxing and letting go of anxiety but as a reliable means of working with the mind: to observe the vicissitudes of mind; to investigate one's identification with their habitual ways of thinking and reacting; to "discover the nature" (a revered Adler phrase) of mind. She'd be aware of the evidence demonstrating that Buddhist-derived meditation over time demonstrably liberates a person's relationship to self, not least by awakening their innate compassion for the suffering of others.

If she were alive today, Stella would come to appreciate

that sitting in silence, noticing the movement as well as momentary stillness of one's mind, softens the clutch of *me*-centricity. Self-glorification, self-cherishing, and self-hatred—another form of self-obsession—all lessen. Basically, in meditation we see that the ego can be tamed, even disenfranchised. When an actor sees through the façade of ego and experiences his own impermanence, he may drop the weight of self-importance. He may let go of the immense effort required to bring attention to his considerable personal assets, including remarkable good looks and charming personality! He may realize his potential to relax into the reality of Artist–Human Being.

Stella advised the actor to recognize that 1) the art of acting is not about him, and 2) the imagination, an attribute of mind, is the most important tool in his arsenal. She accused ego of standing in the way of imagination, insofar as ego revolts against the actor creating characters that aren't replications of itself. Imagination was Stella's forte. She intuitively knew that as ego recedes, imagination expands. If she were alive today, she would discover how meditation enhances imagination and how it awakens real compassion (not idiot compassion) manifesting as honest interest in the lives of others. Benicio del Toro, who called compassion the source of his acting, said his inspiration for work comes from movement, music, and meditation.

Even in my day, Stella seemed to be saying that *me* is both consciously and unconsciously madeup. She intuitively felt, and tried to explain, the ephemerality of *me*. I think, if she were alive today, Stella would fully articulate the prospect that there isn't, within anybody, a solidly reliable, dependably real, identifiable, immutable, locatable, unchanging entity equaling a self. I'm not something solid or pin-down-able. At most, I'm a conglomerate, an ever-changing collection of forms, perceptions, feelings, thoughts, and mental concepts interacting with the world. Or another way of saying it, as is said by quantum physics, is that we are mostly space, with continuously moving parts.

In any case, quite simply, if there was such an entity as a solid self, how could there be the art of acting? In fact, with the art of acting, we have the actor transforming his customary or habitual everyday form, feelings, thoughts, perceptions, and mental concepts into the form, feelings, thoughts, perceptions, and mental concepts of the character that is the role.

In *Listen to Me Marlon*, Brando reveals that his search for an answer to the problem of self (otherwise known as suffering) was unable to be solved by psychotherapy. He turned to introspection and examination of his own mind, sitting in silence. He said, "Until you look inwards, you'll never be able to see clearly outwards." He said he "did a lot of meditation," telling himself, "Don't hang onto thoughts, don't hang onto anything." He came upon "tranquility," through which he found a degree of liberation from the tyranny of self.

Unlike any other kind of artist, the actor can take up a role—fully committed, body and mind—and can drop the role when the show is over and can take up another role. This manifesting and dissolving and manifesting and dissolving and manifesting is the actor's path. Through his mystical, magical ability to disappear into a character, he upends our illusion of a fixed, permanent self. Through the art of transformation, he illuminates the bare truth that we ourselves are like something imagined.

Near the end of Bernardo Bertolucci's 1974 film *Last Tango in Paris*, when the character Jeanne played by Maria Schneider shoots the character Paul played by Marlon Brando, the camera on Brando's face, in a fleeting instant, reveals Brando's communion with Schneider and Paul's communion with Jeanne. Up until the gunshot, Brando has been playing a character named Paul; and Paul, whenever he's with Jeanne, has been playing the role of a made-up self without a name. The moment before the gunshot, Paul is about to end the role of no-name, but then there comes the shot. At the first millisecond of being shot Paul receives the hit and in the next millisecond he comprehends he's been shot. From then on, for Paul, there is only now. He turns from Jeanne, and, seen from behind, weaves his way to the open-air balcony of the apartment where they have been meeting without names. Bertolucci's camera comes around to find Brando/Paul's face as he looks out upon the present moment, and we see life receding from him. Paul loses the look of a man playing a role (as he's been doing with Jeanne the entirety of their time together). With the final hold on Brando/Paul's face, we see that no-name is gone and that Paul is dying; and in some incredible turn of talent, for a moment it seems like Brando is dying, too. In the last image of Paul, he lies in fetal posture on the balcony floor. We're not sorry that the no-name self is gone. We are sorry that the Paul character is dead, just when he was about to stop playing a role. In 1974 we could be glad when the movie was over, knowing that Marlon Brando got up from the balcony and was not dead. But in this day when we rewatch the movie, we know that Marlon Brando, like no-name, is gone, too.

Brando advised actors to "make it as real as you can."

Seeing the truth, he said, will get people to stop chewing popcorn. With *Last Tango in Paris*, Brando momentarily consummated the Artist–Human Being: truthfully performing the actions of a character who is playing a role. While acting out the death of the character, he dissolved the role the character was playing and without pretense also brought the character to his end.

The Actor–Human Being reminds us of our insubstantiality. We appear in this life as a character we imagine, as if onstage; and when our part is over, the curtain comes down. The existence, even the possibility, of the Actor–Human Being makes it infinitely conceivable that when we die, we will take rebirth in some other form. And like an actor, we'll play a new part.

Once and Future Theatre

If you can act you can act anywhere—movies, theatre, on the street, in a church, on any platform.

Stella's orientation was the theatre. Although she performed in Hollywood as a featured player in three major movies, the industry didn't offer her a career. Still, she learned the medium. She considered film less demanding than theatre, less dependent on imagination, less challenging in language, and less collaborative for the actor.

As Kate Mulgrew noted, the movies in which Stella appeared "didn't catch the mystery of her [like they caught the mystery of] Lee Strasberg in *The Godfather*." Mulgrew continued: "Stella did not go back to Hollywood—a mediocre and very profitable way for actors to make a living. Instead, she said, 'I will find my disciples.' And she did. A great teacher is born to be a great teacher."

Stella taught with a mind for theatre as the most deeply human of art forms. In no way did she see theatre as a child of the entertainment industry. Of course, she knew that if a production achieves acclaim, it can be twisted into show business. She likewise knew that the very concept of theatre, as well as the big ideas of plays, may be held in suspicion by members of the public and culturally ignorant public officials. She well knew, in her time, that theatre wasn't rising in popularity in New York City or across the land.

Stella observed that theatre in America has never held the eminent cultural position it enjoys in Europe. She abhorred students' unfamiliarity with signal works of dramatic literature and important actors of the past. She chided students that their reference points for actors and acting were blockbuster movies, television shows, and advertisements. She was saddened by, sometimes angry about, America's theatrical illiteracy.

Stella decried the absence of theatre companies in America for aspirants to join. She agreed with Harold Clurman that what was most lacking in American theatre was a *Theatre*, by which he meant an artistic collective, based on an ensemble of actors giving their utmost, in an ongoing relationship with an audience, altogether providing a sense of social-spiritual unity. Clurman estimated that the Group Theatre playwright Clifford Odets died of cancer because Hollywood, unlike the Group at its best, offered no foundation, no community within which he could fortify and refortify his heart and mind. Clurman similarly attributed playwright William Inge's suicide to the deplorable and crippling American notion that practical success, as in the number of tickets sold, is the measure of talent.

The profit motive on Broadway seems even more dominant in the twenty-first century than it was in the twentieth century of Adler and Clurman. Broadway is home to expensive musicals with super-awesome production values; not many new plays, and scant few classic plays, show up in a New York season; and as for theatres across the country, they are in a severe shrinking mode, as documented by Isaac Butler in his essay "American Theatre Is Imploding before Our Eyes," the opening sentence of which is, "The American theatre is on the verge of collapse." When I asked Kate Mulgrew in 2023 how Stella would feel about the condition of theatre in America today, she replied, "She would find herself very happy to be dead."

In graduate school, I took a course with Harold Clurman called "Theatre Between the Wars." I remember Clurman talking about the hundred-plus plays available on any evening in New York City in the 1920s, with a peak of 297 productions during the 1926–1927 season. On this day that I'm writing in 2024, there are 41 shows on Broadway, musicals dominating by far. The theatre wants playwrights. Actors want playwrights. As Harold Clurman once said to me at a New York opening when I objected to the playwriting: "We need plays, we need more and more new plays, we need plays to provide the manure from which great plays can grow." Where are the playwrights? Where have all the playwrights gone? Gone to content, everyone—content for streaming. Even the movies have gone to streaming.

I recall the story of film director Greta Gerwig asking Meryl Streep to appear in *Little Women*, and Meryl Streep answering, "Yes, I'll be Aunt March. Write me some good lines." Movie actors who are artists long for the language of theatre where, as Stella said, the writer is esteemed.

The challenge to the American playwright, in the words of Harold Clurman, is to make the world's problems his own. But with *me*-memoirs, talk radio and talk TV, reality shows, pundit podcasts, internet forums, and other platforms, there's a prevailing societal impulse to turn one's personal problems over to the world. As Stella contended, among all first-world nations, America has the least regard for theatre's responsibility to society.

I want to call upon the new generation of writers to refocus our attention, directing us toward empathy and away from taking things personally. Dear young writers, you must write for the theatre! It's up to you—courageous and observant playwrights—to respond to the current culture. Let us not forget theatre's ancient origins. We don't want what happened to the theatre in Greece to happen to us wholesale. History informs us that Greek theatre achieved stability and coherence when it turned principally from dance to storytelling. The stories told in Greek plays, taken from legends and a shared mythology, explored the fate of the individual in society. The earliest plays told a story by means of a chorus and one character. Then playwrights increased the number of characters while decreasing the role of the chorus and limited the importance of the supernatural in determining the outcome of a character's actions. Further sophistication led to the depiction of complex characters contending with the principles and conventions upon which Greek society rested. That was the Golden Age of the fifth and fourth centuries BCE. Then Greek playwrighting went into decline, and a celebrity culture emerged to occupy the place of prominence formerly held by the playwright. A system turning individual actors into stars overtook the communal nature of Greek theatre. The values of theatre as a civic forum and a sanctuary for healing disappeared. In her day, Stella Adler gave a warning: a theatre built on a star system offers little more than egotistical entertainment.

Stella Adler kept faith with theatre's superb potential for being a social force, illuminating the human condition. While lamenting the degraded position of theatre in America—"Theatre is a film and television left-over. It's maybe [or maybe not] a permanent situation but it's not a fatal situation."—she exhorted students to reestablish theatre as the main course of the performing arts. She expressed displeasure that established actors had abandoned the theatre for motion pictures and said they must be called back. She argued that there is no screenwriting on the level of playwriting to be found in movies, and not one example of signature writing, except perhaps for Hitchcock. She challenged all actors to "take back the art of acting," becoming an interpretive artist, not just a one-face actor. She herself unto death did not abandon teaching actors about acting.

I'm depending upon the upcoming generation of producers not to replace actors with machines; the upcoming generation of actors not to bypass the stage for video; the upcoming generation of audiences not to abandon live theatre. If we relinquish the theatre, we lose our best chance to publicly share in a live artistic expression of consequence that, whether funny or serious, is capable of effecting a union between players and audience. If we give up on the theatre, where is our opportunity to communally experience empathy; to communally experience artistic representations of people in circumstances other than our own; to communally experience unconventional, uncommon, unclichéd, unsentimental, uneasy, and not untruthful points of view that purvey and weigh the best ideas of our time; and to communally experience a state of integration that relaxes the mind and tenderizes the heart?

The theatre, ideally, beyond any other art, presents a balance between the visible and the invisible. Theatre's primary purpose is not entertainment. It should not exist as noise to block out our grief, as forms of entertainment do. Theatre is not meant as an escape from our lives but a means to observe aspects of our lives more deeply, more fully, more truthfully, that we may do better with them.

I urge young people to grow in confidence. A meditation practice will help with that. Dear young people, the more fearless you are, the more available you'll be to each other and more considerate of, and more touched by, the struggles of others. You'll be kinder, and the content of your theatre will radiate. "To become more alive," Stella said, "observe nature." To be mentally and physically fit for the rigorous routine of acting, she recommended discipline of all kinds—overcoming lazy speech, lazy manners, speediness, emotional breakdowns, bursts of anger, callousness—all in the interest of cultivating the confidence of compassion.

Marlon Brando, in the estimation of Harold Clurman, instead of being an actor, would have rather done some kind of social service for the world, which was in him a wholly authentic impulse, neither pretentious nor phony. He hungered for purification. If only he could have found in the theatre, or in the nearly irredeemable industry of film, a means for being of service! He did genuinely serve in the Civil Rights Movement and on behalf of Native Americans.

But he often dismissed acting as "telling lies." (The mis-understanding that acting is telling lies was first uttered by the lawmaker Solon to Sophocles in Ancient Greece!) It wasn't until very late in life that Brando admitted the work in which he engaged for his entire life was of benefit:

> Many times, I remember being down in the dumps and then I saw a movie that took me away for a few hours and I was completely restored. And I realized, oddly enough, that actors make a contribution to people's lives giving us a gift that you can't buy— something they can imbue with power and beauty and magnificence, something beyond themselves. And we do need that.

According to Clurman, the source of Brando's acting was suffering. The fact that he resisted displaying his own personal suffering on screen, and instead underpinned his roles with the suffering of the character, accounts for his enormously powerful presence.

Dear young people, if you become a stage actor and if you characterize, and on top of that if you take up a contemplative practice to tame the mind, you will begin to care more deeply for all you encounter. The magnanimous stage personality, as Stella called it, may emerge. If you're lucky, magnanimity may likewise emerge if you act in film: see Meryl Streep, see many others. In 1974 I had dinner at an Upper West Side macrobiotic restaurant at a table for two with Al Pacino. Our agenda was to have a conversation about how macrobiotics might be able to help an actor friend of his who was dying of lung cancer. Al Pacino showed up in a trench coat, like Serpico, without pretension. He was funny, maneuvering to eat the Japanese-inspired food, including grains of brown rice, with chopsticks, while asking questions about macrobiotics. He was already a tip-top movie star, and his actor friend was not. His motivation for meeting with me was, "I care." A few days later, reporting how he'd read from a book on macrobiotics to his friend in the hospital, he said, "It was the best cold reading I ever gave." I last saw Al Pacino at the funeral. It was the lifelong experience of both Adler and Clurman that theatre people lean toward altruism, and actors, by nature, are empathic.

Actors need to be employed—they must have a place to work—for their empathy to flourish. A preponderant problem, currently, of theatre in the United States is discontinuity. We lack stable regional theatres with companies of employed actors, and we entirely lack job stability in New York theatre. Without stable companies around the country, stage actors are not hired for season upon season, and they are not necessarily even rehired from one show to another. It's an untenable professional situation.

A CALL TO ACTION

America needs a radically different theatrical model. America needs a theatre for the future. If theatre is to survive, it must find every means possible to take its place, as the Greeks had it, as the highest of performing arts, or the head-and-heart of performing arts, above the sensationalism, conventionality, and falsity that finds its way into television, etc.

I'd like to make two proposals:

- We establish a national theatre, bilocated in New York City as well as another influential urban center, possibly Los Angeles, Chicago, or Washington, DC.

- We establish a multiplicity of theatres across the land—that is, a state theatre in every state's capital or major urban center.

The national theatre would be home to several (five or six or seven) companies of actors—our most accomplished and promising theatre-trained actors, selected to represent the nation as national players. The actors would be cast in productions originating in New York or, say, in LA, and then they would tour. One national company or another would perform a select repertory for a limited run in every state theatre across the land, once or twice a year. The brief residency of the national company at the state theatre may become a beloved momentous occasion!

A national theatre would gradually assemble a repertory of productions of important plays, from classic to modern. (It is stating the obvious to say that a national theatre must operate with artistic independence, including choice and treatment of repertory.) A national company could give a play in their repertoire a new production every tenth season or so, like when the Met will delete an aging staging for a new production of an old opera, or orchestras revive and rework compositions. That's how we may relate to the big ideas in substantial plays: through seeing them more than once. Plays touch us more deeply with repeat viewings. Plays shared across the land can take up residence in our collective consciousness. I remember Stella saying that Russian people in the 1930s went to the Moscow Art Theatre, time and again, to visit with Uncle Vanya or to look in on the three sisters.

A national theatre would need a set of aesthetic, ethical, and societal ideals to be achieved, far beyond the current show-business desire for reviews and salaries. For starters, there is the concept of a group theatre—an interdependent cooperative supporting the ongoing development of its members. A group theatre may be the model for a national theatre company, with the following intentions:

- Cast to talent, not to type, aiming for ensemble acting.
- Engage in shared script interpretation toward the creation of artistically and thematically integrated productions.
- Establish an ongoing continuity of relationship between the theatre group and its audience.
- Aim to affect societal evolution, that is, participate consciously in the emergence of enlightened society.

Theatre isn't a business. It doesn't have to have expensive buildings (though great theatre deserves great playing spaces). It does have to have financial support—sufficient and recurrent. Theatre is an enrichment offering to the people. Theatre in America needs to be subsidized like public libraries, public universities, and public hospitals are subsidized—and all these should receive far more subsidy. (I'm perpetually astonished that gigantic sports facilities—private enterprises bringing in gobs of revenue for their owners and teams—are subsidized with citizen tax monies.) A national American theatre would require government support at the national and state levels as well as the support of wealthy patrons for whom donating money would be a badge of honor, as it was in ancient Greece where wealthy citizens funded the mounting of productions. Greek actors were paid by the state, and their income was supplemented by rich sponsors. In addition to full financing, the future

American theatre, our national theatre, would effectually deserve the psychological support of press and media, and the emotional support of audience appreciation.

Stella Adler believed in the idea of a national theatre. Harold Clurman, across the decades, called for a national theatre. My generation did not answer the call. Nor did my generation's children. There is the generation of my children's children. Who among the young and the very young theatre artists will take up the challenge now? Without a national theatre, I don't know if theatre with integrity will survive in America.

In envisioning a national theatre, the conceivers and makers would do well to consider the origins of theatre, to educate themselves in the history of theatre, and to assess America's place in the lineage of theatre. Even as a national theatre ought to acknowledge history and produce classics, its aesthetics need not have a stuffy or display-case quality. A national theatre may seek to explore societal concerns expressed in great plays from *contemporary* points of view by means of inventive productions. A national American theatre may be about the fate of the nation. It may operate under principles aiming to keep it free of individual self-inflation, aggrandizement, and general see-*me*-ness. It may rely upon wisdom and skillful means to make things better in the world for all beings.

Stella Adler cautioned, time and again, not to want another now, meaning that the actor must want to work with the circumstances given by the playwright. She said, if you know the given circumstances, which includes the partner, you'll know what to do next. Living in the now brings freedom.

It's the same here in the world. We need to know the

circumstances the culture has given us; even as our given circumstances include multiple states of confusion, like believing in the power of stuff, and hurting animals, and harming the natural world, and being ignorant of who we are. Accepting and not rejecting, and not denying, the given circumstances here in the world, we can know what to do next. We can affect the nature of the next now.

Be here now: That may be the actor's slogan. Be here now with confidence: That may be the actor's message. The now is where actors (and Buddhas) reside. The actor living truthfully in the now is the Artist–Human Being. The human being living truthfully in the now creates the future. May the future create an American theatre.

A Stella Adler Chronology

1901: Born in New York City, the youngest daughter of Jacob and Sarah Adler, foremost tragedians of the Yiddish stage.

1906: Made stage debut in her father's production of *The Broken Heart* (Z. Libin) at his Grand Street Theatre; thereafter throughout her childhood she acted with her parents, both here and abroad, in plays by Ibsen, Tolstoy, Hauptmann, and Shakespeare and the Yiddish playwrights Jacob Gordin, S. Ansky, Israel Singer, and Sholem Aleichem.

1919: Made London stage debut at the Pavilion, appearing as Noumi in Jacob Gordin's *Elisa Ben Avia*.

1922: Made English-speaking stage debut on Broadway as the Butterfly in Karel Capek's *The World We Live In* ("The Insect Comedy").

1923: Contracted tuberculosis, forcing her to leave the theatre for about three years.

Mid-1920s: Enrolled for a two-year course at the American Laboratory Theatre, where she met Harold Clurman, and was first exposed to Stanislavsky's new approach to acting, as taught by his disciples Maria Ouspenskaya and Richard Boleslavsky. While studying, she spent two theatre seasons acting with Yiddish theatre stars Jacob Ben Ami and Bertha Kalisch.

1926: Her father, Jacob Adler, died at the age of 71. Close to 100,000 people crowded the streets leading to the Second Avenue theatre where his funeral services were held.

1928: Appreared with all her brothers and sisters in *The Wild Man* by Jacob Gordin.

1931: Joined the Group Theatre, a permanent company co-founded by Harold Clurman, committed to performing new plays that explored American life.

1931: Appeared in Group Theatre's first production, *The House of Connelly* by Paul Green, and in *1931* by Paul and Claire Sifton.

1932: Featured in Group Theatre's production of *Success Story* by John Howard Lawson.

1933: Featured in Group Theatre's production of *Big Night* by Dawn Powell.

1934: Featured in Group Theatre's production of *Gentlewoman* by John Howard Lawson.

1934: Took a leave of absence from the Group and sailed to France for a meeting in Paris with Stanislavsky, which resulted in five weeks of intensive work sessions—and her introduction to, and practice of, a new and more imaginative approach to acting.

1935: Returned to the Group Theatre and began to give her own acting classes, attended by such Group members as Robert Lewis, Sanford Meisner, and Elia Kazan and stressing the principles learned from Stanislavsky.

1935:   Featured in Group Theatre's productions of *Awake and Sing* and *Paradise Lost*, both by Clifford Odets.

1937:   Left for Hollywood when the Group, beset by financial problems and internal discord, canceled its productions for the season.

1939:   Joined the faculty of Erwin Piscator's Dramatic Workshop at the New School for Social Research, where she continued to teach until 1945.

1941:   Appeared in the film *The Shadow of the Thin Man* (MGM).

1942:   Married Harold Clurman.

1943:   Appeared on Broadway in Max Reinhardt's production of *Sons and Soldiers* by Irwin Shaw.

1946:   Appeared on Broadway in a revival of *He Who Gets Slapped* by Leonid Andreyev, directed by Tyrone Guthrie.

1949:   Established the full-faculty Stella Adler Conservatory of Acting, where she then taught for more than 40 years.

1960:   Divorced from Harold Clurman.

1961:   Appeared in London in *Oh Dad, Poor Dad, Mama's Hung You in the Closet and I'm Feeling So Sad*, by Arthur Kopit, her final stage performance.

1966:   Chosen by Robert Brustein to head the acting department at his reorganized Yale School of Drama.

1992:   Died on December 21 at the age of 91.

About the Author

Joanna Rotté is the author of *Scene Change: A Theatre Diary—Prague, Moscow, Leningrad* as well as articles appearing in theatre journals and online arts and culture publications. Rotté is emerita professor of theatre at Villanova University, in Pennsylvania, where she taught acting and script analysis and directed plays for thirty years, including seven years as head of the theatre department. She is a member of Actors Equity. An archive of her writing, performances, and productions may be found at www.joannarotte.com or www.homepage.villanova.edu/joanna.rotte.